The MUGHAL HIGH NOON

Srinivas Rao Adige, educated at the Doon School, Dehradun and St Stephen's College, New Delhi, has worked for the Indian Administrative Service. A keen student of Indian history, he combines his passion for the past with his flair for writing. Adige is married and lives in New Delhi.

The Mughal High Noon is his first novel.

The MUGHAL HIGH NOON

The Ascent of AURANGZEB

SRINIVAS RAO ADIGE

RUPA

Published by
Rupa Publications India Pvt. Ltd 2016
7/16, Ansari Road, Daryaganj
New Delhi 110002

Sales Centres:

Allahabad Bengaluru Chennai
Hyderabad Jaipur Kathmandu
Kolkata Mumbai

This is a work of fiction. All situations, incidents, dialogue and characters, with the exception of some well-known historical and public figures mentioned in this novel, are products of the author's imagination and are not to be construed as real. They are not intended to depict actual events or people or to change the entirely fictional nature of the work. In all other respects, any resemblance to persons living or dead is entirely coincidental.

ISBN: 978-81-291-3726-5

First impression 2016

10 9 8 7 6 5 4 3 2 1

Printed by HT Media Ltd. Noida

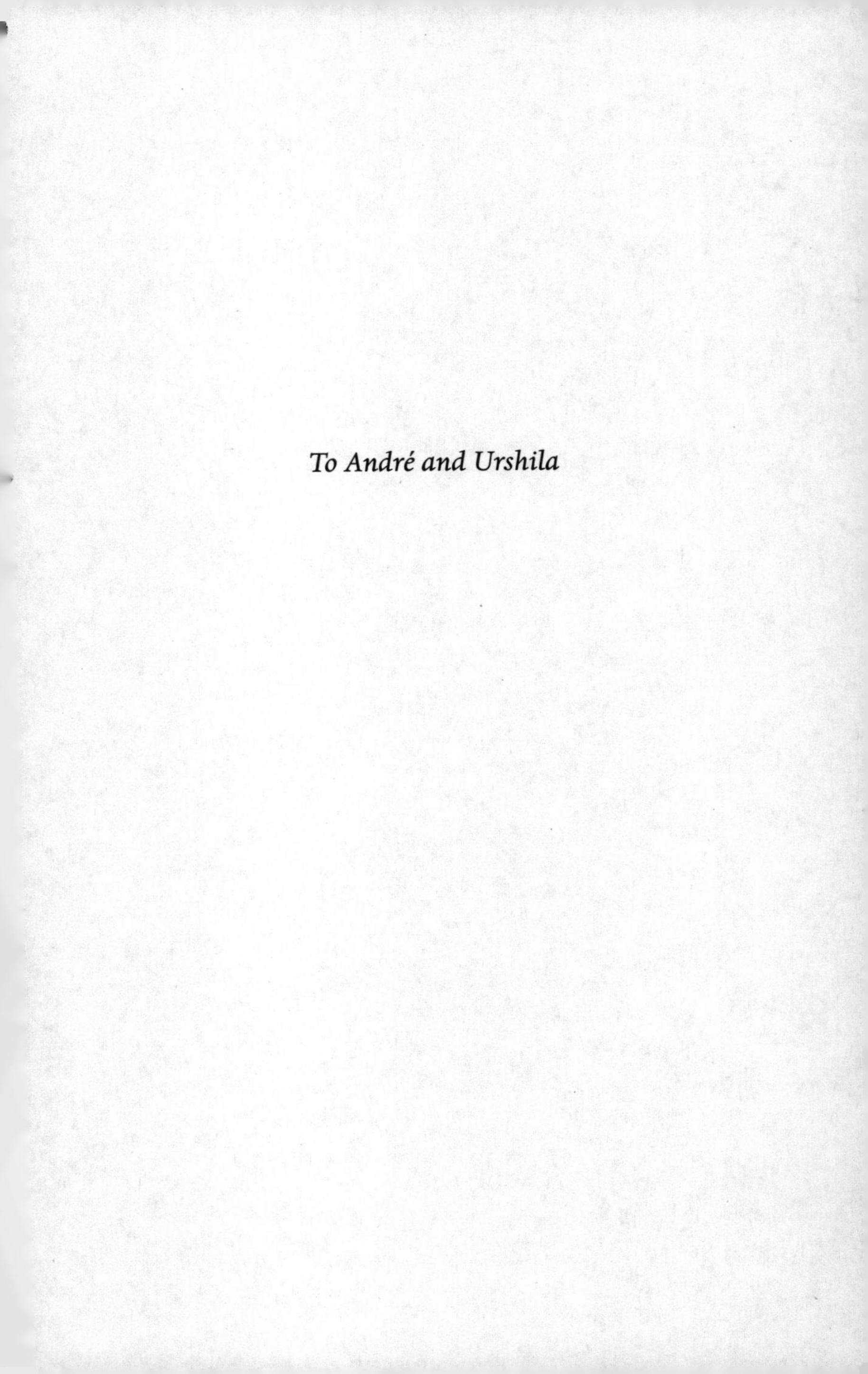

To André and Urshila

One

IT WAS THE middle of the monsoon season. The light breeze that had been blowing since the afternoon had dropped and not a leaf stirred. Dark clouds hung over the imperial city of Delhi. Along its eastern fringes, the waters of the River Jamuna, heavy and swollen at that time of the year from the melting snows of the Himalayas and the monsoon rains, flowed past the massive sandstone walls of the Red Fort, the Quilla-e-Mualla or Exalted Fort, seat of the Mughal emperor Shah Jahan and nerve centre of his empire. Dusk had fallen and amidst the scent of flowers in the gardens surrounding the various exquisitely designed courtyards and pavilions within the fort, the lamp lighters were going about their business, illuminating the corridors and passageways with lighted torches and diyas. In an opulent apartment within a palace in the northern precincts of the fort, Prince Dara Shukoh, the eldest son and heir apparent of the Emperor, sat facing his eldest sister and First Lady of the court, Jahanara Begum. They were talking in low whispers, as if they feared the very walls would hear them.

'The old goat, he knows nothing,' remarked Jahanara Begum, in disgust.

Dara Shukoh looked shocked and said, 'How can you say that? Don't forget, Hakim Allauddin Mirza has fifty years of experience behind him, and he's been treating the royal household since the days of our respected grandfather.'

It was the tenth day since the Emperor's first seizure. The Hakim and his team of physicians were toiling with increasing desperation to cure the Emperor, but with little success. He had not responded to the treatment and his condition had worsened. Swelling had developed in the lower limbs, the throat and palate remained parched, and the body was wracked with high fever. Not a morsel of nourishment had passed through the Emperor's gullet in the last four days, and he lay listlessly upon his bed in the khwabgah, occasionally groaning in pain.

'One year's experience multiplied fifty times doesn't make fifty years of experience,' said Jahanara tartly, creases furrowing her forehead. 'The first seizure which had occurred ten days ago was ascribed to the varak in the zafrani pulao our revered father had consumed the night before he fell ill, the second seizure to strangury and this recent seizure to fluxions in the bowels, but it is clear that his treatment is not working as the attacks are becoming increasingly severe.'

'Don't you think it is too early to lose faith in the treatment? After all, these medicines take time to work. The Hakim has added a course of bloodletting recently, besides tying a specially consecrated amulet, brought from the dargah of Hazrat Nizamuddin Auliya, to father's upper arm,' said Dara tentatively, who always felt a little inadequate before his masterful sister. After all, it was she who had taken over the responsibilities of the First Lady of the court after the death of their mother, Mumtaz Mahal, despite the existence of the Emperor's other three wives.

'Too early did you say? Not only has there been no durbar since the Persian Ambassador's accreditation ceremony on the morning of the first seizure, but for the last four days he has been too ill even to leave the bed or take nourishment. Meanwhile, the court is in complete disarray. Many bazaars have closed down, shops have remained shut fearing breakdown of order, and all sorts of wild rumours are circulating in the city and even beyond, including one that the Emperor is no more.'

'God forbid! We'll personally tear out the tongues of all those who spread such rumours,' said Dara vehemently, as his hand flew to the hilt of his sword. 'In fact, it is to prevent such rumours that we have restricted the access to His Majesty, limiting it to a very few trusted officials, and have also mounted watch on our brothers' agents in court.'

Jahanara didn't say anything immediately. The unspoken truth of the power struggle between the four sons of the Emperor weighed heavily between them.

'Perhaps, it is these very restrictions that are causing such rumours to circulate. If more courtiers were allowed access to the Emperor, the people would know the truth that while no doubt he is ill, he is very much alive. That is a matter for you to think over. However, we came here for a different reason,' said Jahanara. She barely noticed Dara's broad forehead, his lively, intelligent eyes, the long, straight nose, and the generous mouth, but with a chin which, though partially concealed by his beard, receded and betrayed more than a hint of irresolution and indecisiveness.

'What is that?'

'We think it is time we stopped relying on the Hakim's treatment alone, and took a second opinion.'

Dara was taken aback by the suggestion. 'We could try Hakim Shaukat Aziz,' he said. He was not very comfortable with Jahanara's suggestion, but did not want to reject it summarily for fear of offending her, knowing her closeness to the Emperor. 'They say he has a roaring practice. Of course, Mirza Saheb will not like it. You know how these hakims are.'

'We're least concerned with Mirza Saheb's likes or dislikes. Our foremost task is to see that our beloved father recovers swiftly and completely. We feel the course of bloodletting that has been prescribed will weaken the Emperor even further. No, we were thinking of someone else.'

'Who do you have in mind?'

'We'll tell you,' Jahanara whispered. Discreetly throwing a look around them, she continued, 'One of our ladies-in-waiting is Kunwarani Gayatri, granddaughter of Thakur Bhoor Singh of Kalumbar. She told us that her grandfather, who was suffering from the same symptoms, has been cured under someone's medical treatment.'

'If that is so, who is this man? Let's send for him at once,' said Dara, eagerly.

'He's a Hindu, a Brahmin pandit. His name is Ravi Kumar Vaid.'

Dara was stunned. 'A vaid?' he said, his face aghast. 'A non-believer? Do you know what you are saying? How can you even think of having the Emperor treated by a Hindu? Have you considered the political implications of it? If we agree to seek his counsel, and God forbid, suppose something untoward happens, all the ulema and members of the court would be up in arms against us. Only our enemies in court would rejoice. And remember our brothers; Murad in his viceroyalty in Gujarat remains too much in his cups to create trouble and Shuja in Bengal is too far away, but it is Aurangzeb in the Deccan, whom we're most apprehensive about. He will stop at nothing to turn the situation to his advantage.' After a pause he continued, his eyes narrowing, 'And just how did this kunwarani come to know the symptoms of our father's illness? We thought it was a well-kept secret after all the precautions that had been taken.'

'My dear brother,' said Jahanara, pityingly, 'you know very little of what goes on in the palace. The walls here have more holes than the lattice through which we can see the Salimgarh Fort from here. In any case, this is no time to delve into that. With regard to the reaction of our brothers if things go wrong, yes, that is a risk, but it is worth taking considering our father's present condition. A decision has to be taken one way or the other, and that too immediately.'

Dara still looked dubious, and asked, 'What do we know about the vaid?'

'We told you, his name is Ravi Kumar. It is difficult to say where he hails from, but it is believed to be a land deep in the south where the waters of two seas meet, and it's over one month's march even from our brother's capital in Aurangabad. We got this information from Gayatri. From our own inquiries, we gather that he spends a major part of the year in the high Himalayas practising austerities, and collecting rare medicinal plants and herbs. Then he descends to the plains to minister the sick. Since the last month or so, he has been at the residence of Bhai Lakhpati Seth in Asharfi Bazaar, where patients are said to be flocking in droves. Gayatri had told us that her grandfather, who is of the same age as our father, was brought all the way from Kalumbar to Delhi for treatment in a palanquin, as he could neither walk nor ride. But he was back on his feet in a few days because of this man. It is said that his cures are miraculous. It is also said that he, who would barely reach up to your shoulder in height, has the most extraordinary eyes, which seem as if they are looking through one's soul. Having spent a large part of his life in Hindustan, he can speak Farsi as well as Hindustani.'

'We know Lakhpati Seth. This diamond ring that we are wearing was bought from him, when he was last called to the palace to show his wares; though we have never heard of this vaid.'

'That is because you had no occasion to. Well, what is your decision about consulting him?'

'Surely you can't expect me to decide on a matter as important as this so quickly. Remember, this decision may affect the very fate of the empire.'

'Yes, but the consequences of a delayed decision may be equally fatal. In any case, if you want some time to think it over, you shall have it, but let not the decision be postponed indefinitely. Tomorrow morning when you come to the palace, we must sit together and decide. Well, we must get back now as our father's condition may have worsened.'

Dara clapped his hands. A eunuch appeared. 'Jahanara Begum will leave for the palace. Ask her attendants and guards to be ready and have her palanquin summoned. Also, have word sent to alert the guards on duty along the route to the palace.'

The eunuch bowed and then departed to carry out the command. Dara and Jahanara both rose. Jahanara's female attendants came to escort her. Dara looked at his sister with unconcealed affection—her tall, slim figure, and the aristocratic good looks, with the arched eyebrows, the expressive eyes and the full Mughal mouth above a firm jawline. What a pity that the flawless skin of her face was now scarred and puckered beneath the dupatta she wore, owing to that terrible fire incident from which she had barely escaped with her life. She had vowed not to marry and had decided to devote the rest of her life in her father's service.

'Till tomorrow, then,' said Jahanara, as she smiled, turned and left the room with her attendants.

Throughout the night, Dara grappled with Jahanara's suggestion. What if something went wrong, and the Emperor's condition deteriorated even further or worse still, he expired? Would not the blame fall on him? It would not be quite so bad if the second opinion came from a believer. But from a kaffir! A non-believer! The whole empire would be thrown into turmoil. Dara knew that his consorting with Hindus, ordering the translation of the Upanishads into Farsi and his attempts to find common ground between Islam and Hinduism were causing many to accuse him of apostasy. Even the Emperor, who was a judicious ruler and connoisseur of art, had on occasion looked askance at some of these activities. Till now Dara had been able to explain it away as being motivated by his abiding thirst for knowledge, a thirst which his faith encouraged, but this was something altogether different. To allow an unbeliever to touch the Emperor's body was bad enough. If the kaffir's treatment failed and the Emperor died, the consequences would be infinitely worse. The entire body of the ulema, the great nobles, his own brothers, as well as his other sister Roshanara, would be ranged against him. And as surely as day followed night, he would be declared unfit to wield the sceptre as Shah Jahan's heir. He might even be accused of parricide.

Yet, was there any other alternative? Was not Jahanara telling the plain, unvarnished truth when she said that Hakim Allauddin Mirza's treatment was not working? Would not Hakim Shaukat Aziz's treatment only be more of the same? After all were they not from the same school of Yunani medicine? If the present treatment continued, what chance had the Emperor of surviving, considering that his strength was ebbing by the hour? If indeed the vaid was reputed to effect miraculous cures, what was the harm in giving it a try? If the Emperor failed to respond, the hakims could always be called back; and in case the Emperor recovered fully, the credit would be completely ours. Not only would this mean renewed confirmation of our succession to the throne, but it would give added weight to our counsel and strengthen the force of our decrees in the future.

As these thoughts swirled in Dara's mind, he fell into a fitful sleep.

At dawn, Dara set out from his apartments for the emperor's palace in the Red Fort, with his escort. After crossing a series of courtyards and pavilions, he reached the Diwan-e-am, where he asked his escort to retire. Then passing through a pair of ornately decorated gates, he entered a long corridor that led to the Emperor's private apartments within the palace.

Reaching Shah Jahan's bed in the khwabgah, Dara found the Emperor lying and breathing heavily. His face was bathed in perspiration and looked drawn, with the lips parched and cracked. Occasionally a groan escaped his lips. Jahanara sat at the foot of the bed, pressing his legs, a look of deep concern etched on her face. Two eunuchs stood behind the bedhead alternately fanning the Emperor.

'We want privacy,' commanded Dara. The eunuchs slunk away.

'How is he?' Dara whispered.

'There's been no improvement since last evening. Hakim Saheb came with a couple of other palace physicians a short while ago. He has now prescribed a decoction with the addition of mercury. This, he said, would effectively restore the balance in the humours. He went to bring the ingredients, and said that he would be back soon.' Jahanara took a golden goblet half-filled with water, and held it to the Emperor's lips. As he made no effort to sip it, she dipped her forefinger into it and moistened his lips.

'Well, have you thought over the suggestion we made last evening?' she asked.

Dara signalled to her to come with him to a corner of the room. Jahanara rose and followed him.

'Don't you think we should consult some of the others? What about Roshanara? We could wait till she returns.'

At the mention of her sister's name, Jahanara's jaw tightened. There was little love lost between the two, as both were competing for the Emperor's affections and thus far Jahanara was clearly the winner. Roshanara, who was considered to be close to the faction which did not support Dara in court, had gone to Kashmir to get away from the burning heat of Delhi's summer. There she had been informed of the Emperor's illness and was hastening back to Delhi, but was still some days' march away.

'There's not enough time for that. A decision has to be taken today itself, by the time the sun has reached its zenith, and in any case, latest by sunset.'

'What about Akbarabadi Begum then? At least she could be consulted?' asked Dara, desperate that he alone should not be called upon to take such a momentous decision. She was the senior-most of the Emperor's wives, and could possibly be of some help.

'You know that she is practically demented. We don't know whether she can even distinguish between light and darkness. It would be worse than useless to consult her,' replied Jahanara.

'Then what about some of the senior courtiers or nobles?'

Jahanara was getting exasperated. 'What are you going to ask them? Whether a Hindu vaid can be allowed to treat the Emperor? What do you expect them to say?' she whispered fiercely.

The Emperor groaned. Jahanara rushed to his side, brushed his lips with water and pressed his legs for a little while, before joining Dara again. 'When is this wretched Hakim Saheb returning with the ingredients? As we were saying, what answer do you expect? Some may agree, but the majority will disagree. In the meantime, the entire court will come to know about it, and in a trice it will spread throughout the empire that the Emperor is being treated by a Hindu. If, God forbid, anything untoward happens, can you imagine what capital people like our brother Aurangzeb will make of it? They will say that we got the Emperor poisoned, and by a Hindu at that. There will be no place on earth for you and me to hide. No, the decision will have to be taken by the two of us alone.'

'That's exactly what we're afraid of. Only the two of us taking the decision, and facing the consequences if things go wrong.'

'As we pointed out last evening, that's a risk we have to take. But that is better than watching our beloved father's condition deteriorate by the hour. In any case, we're sure that nothing will go wrong.'

'How can you be so sure? Suppose this Gayatri has been

planted by our enemies, and is feeding this information to us merely to lead us into a trap? Any of our brothers could be involved in this. Even Roshanara could have arranged to have this maid feed you with this story of her grandfather being cured by this vaid and made it a point to be away from Delhi during this period, so that no suspicion should fall on her.'

The Emperor groaned again. Jahanara flew to his side and then looking at the water clock that stood close by, she poured out a greenish blue liquid from a bottle into the golden goblet, and then dipping her fingers into it, she moistened the Emperor's lips. 'That wretched Hakim, shuffling along at an ant's pace. When will he return?' she asked Dara.

'If he had gone some time ago, he should be on his way back now', said Dara consolingly.

'We think your suspicions are unfounded. We're sure Gayatri is telling the truth and this is no trap,' replied Jahanara. 'Remember, she's the granddaughter of a Thakur, who belongs to the Rathore clan of Rajputs, for whom their word is their bond. We have no reason to disbelieve her. In any case, why should she feed us with false information? To be doubly sure, we got her to swear on the head of her dead father and also told her that we knew a secret of hers, which if it got to the ears of her grandfather, would mean her certain death at his hands.'

'What's that?' asked Dara, his curiosity aroused.

'That's no concern of yours,' retorted Jahanara sharply. Then, looking at her brother's face etched with doubts, she softened and added, 'It concerns a young nobleman who belongs to our faith. It is enough if we say that she is completely under our thumb, and we know what she's saying is the truth. Meanwhile, after coming back to the palace last evening, we got further inquiries made about this Vaid from our own sources, and all of them speak very highly of his curative powers.'

'But a Hindu!' expostulated Dara. 'Can you imagine a Hindu entering the Emperor's private apartments, and even touching the Emperor's person?' Dara felt that he was losing the battle with Jahanara.

'Ssssshhhhh!' Jahanara whispered. 'Do you want to wake up the dead? As far as him being a Hindu is concerned, remember the Hakim's medicines are not working, and the Emperor's life is ebbing away before our very eyes. Let us not forget that some part of Hindu blood flows in our veins too, and among the various doctors called to treat us during our burn injury, at least one was a Hindu. Illness and pain know no religion, and in any event, desperate situations call for desperate remedies. At this rate, the Emperor will assuredly breathe his last and our brothers are bound to contest the succession. We have to do everything in our power to ensure that the Emperor recovers fast. We know you have the Emperor's welfare at heart, as much as we have, and that's why we have made this suggestion to you.' Jahanara stood up and grasped Dara's shoulders, and looked him squarely in the eye. 'As the Emperor's eldest son, the decision is now for you to take. We can come with you only this far.'

Just then there was the shuffle of feet in the corridor outside. 'Hakim Allauddin Mirza begs entrance,' announced a eunuch, entering the chamber.

'We'll be behind the curtain,' said Jahanara, leaving the room from the opposite end.

Dara nodded. 'Show Hakim Saheb in,' he said.

Hakim Allauddin Mirza was an ancient wisp of a man. His eyes were rheumy, and a straggly beard ran down the side of his cheeks, reaching his waist. His fingers were almost skeletal as he shuffled forward in his ankle-length robe, holding a flagon in one hand and a small box in the other. He was accompanied by an assistant. He bowed to Dara, and then proceeded to the Emperor's bedhead.

'The Emperor is practically delirious, Hakim Saheb,' said Dara. 'Jahanara Begum, who was here a little while ago, tells us that there has been no improvement in his condition since last night, and if anything, his condition has worsened. So many days have gone by now. Are you sure you are on the right track?'

'In matters of sickness, we cannot be sure of anything, Your Highness,' replied the Hakim, in a querulous voice. 'Medical science teaches us that the cause of all illness is imbalance in the humours and all that we can do is attempt to set right that imbalance. As the original imbalance was caused because of the varak used in the zafrani pulao, leading to strangury, complicated by fluxions in the bowels, and the earlier medicines having failed, I now propose to administer him a decoction composed of mint, cardamom and fennel to which some mercury has to be added, which is said to be highly efficacious in cases such as this.'

'But this is the eleventh day since the first seizure!' protested Dara. 'Whatever be the cause of the imbalance, surely eleven days is time enough for it to be righted. You're seeing the Emperor's condition. Instead of improving, it is steadily deteriorating. How confident are you that this mixture of mercury and the decoction will work, when your other medicines haven't?'

The Hakim avoided a direct answer. 'I have also brought another special amulet with me consecrated at the dargah of Hazrat Nizamuddin Auliya to be tied to the Emperor's upper arm. Its efficacy would be greatly enhanced if a flawless white diamond were procured and placed in the Emperor's right hand to draw out the bile. Meanwhile, I shall administer the mixture to the Emperor.'

Pouring the decoction from the flagon into a small cup, he added the mercury taken from a phial in the box to it, stirred it and then held a spoonful of the mixture to the Emperor's lips. As the mouth remained firmly clenched, the Hakim tried to prise it open gently with the spoon, but most of the mixture dribbled onto the Emperor's beard.

'This is to be repeated at every watch,' said the Hakim. 'Now I shall tie the amulet.' Uttering a few words of prayer, he tied it to the Emperor's upper arm. 'I shall be back after two watches, Your Highness. My assistant, who has been specially trained by me, and whose competence I can vouch for, will remain outside. Meanwhile, please procure the white diamond. I hope to see some improvement in His Majesty's condition by the time I return.' Slowly, the old man shuffled out.

After the Hakim and his assistant had left the chamber, Jahanara emerged from behind the curtain and resumed her seat by the emperor's bed, gently dabbing the perspiration from his forehead with her dupatta.

'See what we mean? Does he inspire any confidence in you? He didn't give you a straight answer when you asked him how confident he was that this new treatment would work.'

'Well he said he hoped to see some improvement within two watches,' Dara countered defensively, standing by her side.

'Rubbish! The man himself is a walking corpse. A few doses of this new mixture and whatever little life subsists in our beloved father will be extinguished.'

'What do you propose then?'

'What we've been saying all along since last evening. Send for this vaid. Assess him. See if you feel comfortable in assigning the Emperor's treatment to him.'

'What if Hakim Saheb and others find out?'

'No one need ever know. Hakim Saheb has himself said that a flawless white diamond has to be placed in the Emperor's hand. Send for this Lakhpati Seth, saying that you want to buy a white diamond to match one or two already with you. When he comes, tell him to fetch the vaid to treat a Hindu in your entourage, who has suddenly taken ill and cannot be moved. Do all this from your apartments within the fort itself. When the vaid comes, we will devise a plan to bring him here.'

'Suppose the Emperor refuses to be treated by this vaid?'

'In his present condition, the Emperor can hardly recognize anybody, least of all which religion he professes. What we have to do is to get a correct diagnosis and the medicines required. The rest we can do ourselves. The vaid needs to see the Emperor only once, or at best twice, for that.'

'How are you going to smuggle him past all the guards, attendants, officials and eunuchs?'

'Leave that to us. Once he reaches your apartments within the fort, it will be our job to get him to these chambers undetected.'

'What if he refuses to treat the Emperor? Why should he want to stick his neck out, when the consequences of failure might mean even death?'

'We've been told that as in the case of our Yunani physicians, it is in their code never to refuse to treat someone who is unwell, and we are sure he would not like to breach that. Moreover to cure the Emperor of Hindustan, when others have failed, must surely represent the professional challenge of a lifetime. However otherworldly he may be, in his own conscience at any rate, he would not like to see himself as having refused it.'

Dara said nothing. He leaned forward a little, looking at Jahanara's pale distraught face. There was palpable silence in the room, broken only by the Emperor's laboured breathing.

'Very well,' muttered Dara at last. 'We are not at all sure whether this plan of yours will work, but we are willing to take the risk on two conditions. Firstly, before we let this vaid anywhere near the Emperor, we will meet him and satisfy ourselves that he inspires confidence. Secondly, if within a day or at most two, the vaid's treatment leads to no improvement, we shall go back to the Hakim's treatment, supplemented by the advice of any other physician he would like to consult. Of course, this will remain entirely confidential between us, and if the Emperor does recover with the vaid's treatment, it will be announced that Hakim Saheb was responsible for the recovery. Agreed?'

'Done,' said Jahanara, smilingly as she looked up at Dara. Then she added softly, 'We still remember how our respected father sat up night after night, dressing our bandages with his own hands after the fire incident, and all that amidst the burdens of empire. This is only a small token of our recompense.'

'Very well, then. Let's do it this way. We shall send for Lakhpati Seth and ask him to bring the vaid to meet us in our apartments before sundown. If the vaid passes muster, we shall send you a message containing the phrase "Allah-u-Akbar". It will then be up to you to arrange to get the vaid from our apartments to this chamber undetected, so that he can examine the Emperor, and then he will have to be escorted back to my apartments, from where we will arrange for his return to Lakhpati's residence. The examination can be arranged at twilight. Either one of us, or preferably both, must be present during the examination.'

'Very well, we will be awaiting your message,' said Jahanara.

Dara instructed the eunuchs and the Hakim's assistant, who were in the corridor, to let him know immediately if there was any change in the Emperor's condition, and then proceeded to his own apartments in the fort. On reaching there, he sent for Lakhpati Seth.

Soon the rotund jeweller, with a round face and merry eyes, appeared before Dara.

'To what do I owe the honour of being summoned, Your Highness?' he asked, bowing before Dara.

'Ah! There you are, Sethji. We are looking for a flawless white diamond because as you know, the Emperor is indisposed, and his physicians have advised that the holding of such a diamond in his hand will assist in his recovery.'

'I believe I have just the diamond Your Highness seeks. May I fetch it for inspection?'

'Do so. We are also told that a famous vaidji is residing with you. A pandit, who is translating the Upanishads into Farsi in our library has suddenly been struck with convulsions and cannot be moved. Do you think the vaid could come and have a look at him? Needless to say he will be well recompensed for his trouble.'

Lakhpati bristled slightly. 'Vaidji does not treat patients for money, Your Highness. He does it out of compassion for the suffering. However, I don't see why not. I'll have to ask him, of course.'

'Excellent. Then please go and fetch the diamond, and if not inconvenient, also bring the vaidji along with you.'

Dara clapped his hands, and a eunuch appeared immediately. 'Have Sethji escorted to his residence. When he returns, have the guards at the gate informed that he and any person with him should be allowed to enter.'

The eunuch bowed and the Seth followed him out.

It was nearing sundown, and Dara's impatience was mounting, when the Seth was announced. He came bustling in with another man in tow. 'Vaidji had gone to some neighbouring villages to treat the patients there, and returned only a short while ago. I have brought him and also the diamond with me.'

Dara glanced at the jewel merchant, but it was the other man who attracted his attention. He was very short, but slim and wiry, with a complexion the colour of ripened wheat and a body that seemed to radiate energy and good health. The head was beautifully shaped with a broad forehead, surmounted by snow-white, close-cropped hair, but it was the man's eyes which were his most arresting feature. They were grey in colour, with enormous irises, and their gaze was unwavering. He was dressed in a simple white cloth, wrapped over his body, with wooden clogs on his feet.

'Welcome, Vaidji,' said Dara affably, showing him and the jewel merchant to a divan by his side, as he took his seat opposite them. 'We have heard so much about you. We hope you have not been inconvenienced?'

'It is an honour to be remembered by Prince Dara, whose effulgence lights up the four corners of world,' said the Vaid courteously, in passable Farsi.

Dara smiled. 'You speak Farsi admirably. We shall be with you in a trice.' Then turning to the Seth, he said, 'Well Sethji, let us see the diamond.'

Lakhpati Seth drew out a small string bag, and took out a big white diamond. Dara took the diamond and went to the window, and held it against the fading light to examine it closely. 'Yes, we think this will do admirably. What is its cost?'

'Ninety thousand gold mohurs, Your Highness.'

Dara walked up to a large rosewood cupboard in a corner of the room. He took out a velvet bag and opened it. 'Well, this bag seems to contain about a lakh of mohurs. It goes with your name,' he chuckled. 'Please go into the next room and count it. If it is less than ninety thousand let us know. If it is more, let it be adjusted against future purchases.'

Seth happily went to the adjoining room with the bag.

Dara then turned to the Vaid. 'A pandit translating the Upanishads…' he began. The Vaid at once held up his hand. Dara stopped. The Vaid looked steadily into Dara's eyes.

'Surely, Your Highness, you don't expect me to believe that you have summoned me here just to examine your pandit,' said the Vaid.

Dara was dumbstruck. His eyes widened in amazement. 'In truth, no,' he murmured, after a pause. 'But how did you know?'

The Vaid did not reply, but looked on at Dara, a smile on his lips and his gaze unrelenting.

'It is the Emperor,' Dara at last blurted. 'He has been severely ill these last eleven days, and his condition worsens by the hour. The hakims who are treating him, led by Allauddin Mirza, the chief palace physician, have diagnosed the case to be one of strangury, complicated by fluxions in the bowels. His Majesty has been having acute pain in the lower abdomen, his hands and feet have swollen and his throat is parched. He has been running high fever and has had no nourishment for the last four days. On the day of the first seizure eleven days ago, he was administered a purgative, which gave him a little relief. But three days later, he had a second seizure and then a third one. Since then, he has not risen from his bed. When we saw him this morning, he was practically delirious. The hakims had initially put the malady down to the consumption of some varak, that was used to cover the zafrani pulao, he had eaten the night before the first seizure, which contained impurities, and prescribed several medicines. Later, they prescribed bloodletting but even that did not do any good. They are now administering a decoction to which mercury has been added, but we have our doubts whether this remedy will work either. Could we request you to have a look at him?'

'Would Hakim Saheb like another person, and that too belonging to another faith, intruding into his preserve? Even if we belong to different schools of medicine, we have our ethics, you know.'

'He need never know about it,' Dara mumbled.

'You mean I have to go through the corridors and pathways of the fort, examine the Emperor in secret, and then hopefully set him on the road to recovery, without Hakim Saheb, or anyone else knowing?' He laughed delightedly, and clapped his hands like a child. Suddenly, he became serious. 'And suppose the Emperor refuses to be treated by me, or I am unable to cure him, what then?'

'As for the first, the Emperor at present is barely conscious and unable to recognize anyone. Regarding the second, if you fail, we revert to the original line of treatment.'

The Vaid thought for a moment. 'I see. Very well, I will see him,' he said.

'Then, you agree?'

'Do I have a choice?' replied the Vaid, smiling.

'Excellent. Please remain seated here, while arrangements are made for you to examine the Emperor.' Dara got up and swiftly went into the adjoining chamber. Snatching a piece of parchment, he wrote, 'All is well. Allah-u-Akbar!' Sealing it, he clapped his hands. A eunuch appeared. 'Give this to Jahanara Begum. She will be in her apartments. If it is not in her hands within a quarter of this watch, we shall personally shorten you by a head.'

The eunuch fled with the note. Dara returned to where the vaid was seated. 'It will take only a little while,' he said. He was now not the heir to the wealthiest empire in the world, but a son wracked by anxiety as to whether his father would survive or not.

'How long have you been treating patients?' asked Dara, by way of making conversation.

'For the last fifty-eight years. I am 76 years old now. At the age of 10, my preceptor initiated me into Yoga and Ayurveda. For the next eight years, I simply watched him, and helped him by performing menial tasks, before he allowed me to treat patients, on my own, under his supervision of course, beginning with the simplest cases.'

'We've seen these ascetics performing some of the most marvellous yogic feats during our early morning rides along the River Jamuna, and also during the Kumbh at Allahabad. They can bend and twist their bodies into the most amazing contortions. Sometimes they do so for a few coins below the palace walls here.'

The Vaid laughed. 'Those postures are the relatively simpler part of yoga. Many of those who perform these feats are humbugs and charlatans. Yoga is derived from the Sanskrit word "yukta" and means union—to unite with God. To realize God, you need to have a healthy body. You can hardly focus your attention on God if you are plagued with a persistent backache can you? These postures or "asanas" as we call them are merely a means of maintaining a healthy, disease-free body so that you are not distracted by it in your search for God. For this purpose a few basic asanas are more than sufficient, without the need for all those contortions.'

'And Ayurveda?'

'That is no different. Ayurveda means "the science of life". The prevention and cure of disease is only one aspect of it. It can go far beyond that and help you increase your life span, treating age as the greatest disease. A whole ocean of knowledge lies behind these disciplines, and I for all my years, still feel like a child on the banks of that ocean.'

'Fascinating,' murmured Dara.

Just then there was a discreet cough behind one of the lattices.

'We shall be back in a moment,' Dara said. He went behind the lattice. A eunuch was standing there, waiting for him.

'Yes?'

'Jahanara Begum is waiting in the inner courtyard, Your Highness' the eunuch said.

Dara returned to the Vaid and said, 'Please remain seated here. We shall be back immediately.'

Dara went down to the courtyard. Jahanara was standing there, wearing a burka.

'So, what do you think about him?' she asked, excitedly.

'Truly amazing! If there is anyone who can cure the Emperor, we feel it is this man. How do we get him now to the Emperor's apartments?'

'Where is he now?'

'In our apartments.'

'We've brought a spare burka for him. We will ask him to wear it and then smuggle him to the Emperor's apartments. You don't think he'll mind, do you?'

'No. In fact, he laughed at the idea of going to examine the Emperor in secret.'

'Well, if that firangi Manucci, and the earlier one, what's his name…yes Tavernier, could be smuggled in disguise, right inside the harem, we don't see why the vaid cannot be brought to the Emperor's chamber in a burka,' replied Jahanara.

Both of them entered Dara's apartments and went up to the chamber where the Vaid was waiting.

'We regret to have kept you waiting, Vaidji,' said Dara. 'We will have to adopt a subterfuge to get you to the Emperor's chamber, to avoid prying eyes. You don't mind wearing this burka, do you? It will only be for a short while.'

'Not at all. I will then have acquired at least one aspect of divinity,' said the Vaid laughingly. 'I will be able to see the world, but the world will not be able to see me.'

Donning the burka and leaving his clogs behind, he followed the two through a maze of darkened, less-frequented passages and courtyards to the Emperor's chamber, just as the lamps were being lit throughout the palace. Shah Jahan lay on the bed, quite still and it was obvious that his condition had deteriorated during the course of the day. His fever had risen, and he made a rasping sound each time he drew breath.

'We desire privacy,' commanded Dara. The eunuchs and the Hakim's assistant, who were huddled in a corner of the chamber, melted away.

The Vaid removed his burka and went up to the Emperor's

bedhead. Taking a lamp, he looked closely at the Emperor's face, noting the pallor, the rasping breath and the dryness of the lips. He examined the undersides of the eyelids, and prising open the Emperor's mouth, he peered down the gullet. He felt the pulse and after loosening the undershirt, tapped at the Emperor's chest and palpitated his abdomen and lower stomach carefully, with his strong, spatulate fingers. He examined the Emperor's hands and feet, paying particular attention to the colour of the nails and the skin at the extremities. Dara noted the complete confidence with which the Vaid went about his job.

His examination over, the Vaid took the brother and sister to a corner of the chamber. 'His condition is indeed serious, but he will recover,' he said. 'I will send two Ayurvedic medicines, when I get back. The dosage will be marked on the bottles, which is to be administered four times a day, beginning tonight. First the medicine in the bigger bottle has to be consumed, and then the one in the smaller bottle. Some improvement can be expected by tomorrow evening itself, and he should be well on the road to full recovery within a week. He will remain weak of course, and for a fortnight or so he should be kept on a light diet, consisting mainly of vegetables and fruits. Thereafter, he may resume his normal diet, though it is advisable to avoid heavy curried meat. Other medicines should be stopped immediately. I don't think it is necessary for me to examine him again, but if there is any need, you know where to find me. I shall be in Delhi for the next forty-five days.'

A flicker of embarrassment crossed Dara's face. 'This visit will remain completely confidential, of course.'

The Vaid looked at the two with kindness and said, 'Have no fear. I shall not reveal to anymore about this visit. Many of the nobles and the ulema would no doubt turn violent if they came to know that the Emperor of Hindustan was being treated by a kaffir. Some of my own people would look askance at me if they knew that I had as much as touched a mlechha, even if he is the Emperor. Narrow-mindedness and obscurantism are not the monopoly of a single community.'

A wave of relief swept over Dara and Jahanara at the confident optimism and tact displayed by this extraordinary little man.

'How can we ever thank you, Vaidji?' asked Dara. 'Would you be good enough to accept jewels, gold, land, the revenues of villages?'

'It is too early to thank me. Let His Majesty begin to recover first. After that, if you want to thank me, nothing would please me more than for you to open an orphanage for the children of those killed in battle, who have none to look after them, regardless of religion, caste or creed. There they should be taught the principles espoused by your glorious ancestor, the Emperor Akbar, whom I had the good fortune to see as a young boy in Prayag.'

Two

MIR NASRULLAH KHAN paced the floor of his palace in Delhi's Daryaganj area. An important decision was weighing on his mind.

He was a mansabdar of five thousand horsemen at the Imperial Court, but he was also the master spy of Prince Murad Baksh, youngest of the Emperor's four sons and Viceroy of Gujarat. It was presently his duty to apprise his paymaster of the Emperor's actual medical condition, amidst the rumours that were swirling around the capital. The rumours were worsened by Dara's barring access to the Emperor, his censorship of news and his efforts to ensure that only his own soothing version of the Emperor's medical condition reached his brothers in their viceroyalties. He knew that the residences of the officially accredited agents of Prince Shuja, Prince Aurangzeb and Prince Murad at court were under tight surveillance; their incoming letters were being secretly opened and read. Official couriers carrying their mail were being regularly intercepted by Dara's mobile patrols, some of whom had even been murdered. That source of information having been effectively closed to his master, the Mir knew that a daunting responsibility rested on his shoulders. Any slip-up might cost Murad the throne, but would certainly cost the Mir his head.

The matter for decision was the degree of credence to be attached to the information brought to him that afternoon by Chanda (one of Dara's eunuchs who was in the Mir's pay) that a Hindu vaid had been taken secretly to examine the Emperor, two days earlier, as a result of which the Emperor was improving, and was expected to recover in a fortnight or so.

'How can you be so sure that he was a Hindu?' asked the Mir for the third time.

'As I mentioned, Your Excellency, this jeweller Lakhpati Seth visits Prince Dara from time to time, with gems for approval,' Chanda simpered.

'So?'

'My Lord asked the Seth to show him a flawless white diamond and also asked him to bring along this vaid who is treating patients at the Seth's residence, on the pretext that one of the pandits working in his library had suddenly taken ill. Then, the Seth brought a Hindu man, which was clear from his dress and the caste marks on his forehead.'

'What is this vaid's name?'

'I couldn't catch it, Your Excellency, as I was suddenly called away, but later when I was passing behind a lattice, I heard Lord Dara requesting the vaid that evening to examine the Emperor and prescribe suitable treatment, as Hakim Saheb's treatment was not working. The vaid agreed.'

'Describe this vaid to me.'

'He is of short stature. He would barely reach up to Your Excellency's shoulders. White hair, piercing eyes, dressed in a dhoti, wore wooden clogs, speaks Farsi reasonably well, but with an outlandish accent.'

'Then what happened?'

'Jahanara Begum came to Prince Dara's apartments within the fort. She had brought a spare burka with her. They made this vaid wear the burka, and were mentioning amongst themselves that they would take him through some of the less-frequented passages to the Emperor's apartments.'

'Was he wearing his clogs too?'

'No, Your Excellency. He left his clogs behind in my Lord Dara's chamber. I was alone in the room and tried to put them on, but they were too small and uncomfortable.' The eunuch giggled.

The Mir felt sickened at the eunuch's falsetto voice, but persisted in the conversation. Too much was at stake.

'Then what happened?'

'About half a watch later, my Lord Dara and this vaid returned to the chamber. My Lady stayed back. The vaid then took off the burka, which My Lord stuffed into a nearby box.'

'Where were you at the time?'

'I was pouring water into some plants behind the lattice, Your Excellency.'

'Did you spend all your time behind the lattice?'

'Excellency, if creatures like this humble self were not there, who would give precious nuggets of information to Lords like yourself?'

'Hmmmppphhh...then what happened?'

'When the vaid was back in his normal attire, a pandit who is working in Lord Dara's library was brought to be examined by the vaid. That was only an excuse to explain the vaid's presence there, as the pandit was suffering only from mild biliousness. I heard the vaid prescribing some medicines, and then he was escorted out.'

'So you did not see the vaid actually entering the Emperor's chamber and administering any medicines to him?'

'No, Your Excellency. My duties are confined to Lord Dara's apartment, in the fort complex.'

'Then on what basis do you say that the Emperor is recovering because of the vaid's treatment?'

'I'm only putting two and two together. A vaid is brought to my Lord Dara and Lady Jahanara. He agrees to examine the Emperor. My Lord and Lady say that they will take him to the Emperor's chamber. A spare burka is made available. He is gone for half a watch. He leaves his clogs behind. Since yesterday, the Emperor's condition is said to be improving. The inference is irresistible.'

'Hmmmm...Have you told this to anyone?

'None, Your Excellency. I came straight to you.'

'You have done well.'

The eunuch caught the purse full of gold mohurs thrown at him, peered into it, smiled and looked up.

'Speak of this to no one, understand? If a word of this gets out, I will chase you even if you are in hell. Already you lack...' the Mir glanced below the eunuch's waist. 'Be careful that you do not lose your neck as well.'

The eunuch bowed and departed. The Mir pondered over the eunuch's statement. Was it true? Was the Emperor's condition really improving? Was the person who had come to the royal window to give audience this morning really the Emperor, or had Dara got somebody to impersonate him, as many were saying? Could a vaid succeed where the most eminent Hakims in the realm had failed? Could a kaffir, an unbeliever, penetrate the most closely guarded chamber in the world? Weighty questions! The answers could shake the very roots of the empire! The world knew that amongst the Mughals, the law of primogeniture was followed more in the breach than in the observance. It was Takht-Ya-Takhta (the crown or the plank situation). If indeed the Emperor was no longer alive, the prompt delivery of the information would give Prince Murad invaluable lead time to collect funds, marshal his forces and mount an assault on Delhi. If on the other hand the Emperor was recovering, any such activity would be considered rebellion, whose consequences would be catastrophic. The Mir would therefore have to exercise the utmost care in analysing the facts while drafting his secret report to Murad. One wrong word, and his life would be snuffed out by Murad's assassins, lurking in the by-lanes of Delhi, for having misled the Viceroy. In the Mughal world, there were no second chances.

He decided not to take a chance and checkout the vaid for himself.

Well before dawn, the Mir slipped out of his residence. He had donned the coat of an ordinary Mughal trooper above his own clothes and had wrapped a shawl around his shoulders. Skirting the giant Jumma Masjid on its eminence, he at length reached the jeweller's precinct in Asharfi Bazaar.

Walking into the narrow street leading to Lakhpati Seth's haveli, the Mir saw a clutch of people, many of whom were elderly and sick, being led into and out of a gate that opened out on to the street. Going up to the gate and peering in, he found that it led to an open courtyard in which a number of people were squatting, patiently waiting for their turn to be treated by a tiny man with white hair. The Mir entered the courtyard and stationed himself behind a pillar in the gallery that ran all round the yard, trying to make himself as inconspicuous as possible, as he watched the vaid deal with his patients for quite a while and heard the hubbub of conversation all round him.

'What is your ailment? Are your hakims not able to cure you?'

The Mir looked down to his right. Seated on the floor of the gallery was a wizened old man in a dirty white dhoti, with gnarled hands and feet, holding a wooden stave.

'Nothing's the matter with me,' replied Nasrullah, his face muffled with the shawl. 'I have come looking for a certain Rawat Singh. We were together in the Balkh campaign, and he had sent word to me that he would be coming to consult the vaid here this morning for his ague. I thought it a good opportunity to meet him after all these years.'

'This is the hour which vaidji devotes to the poor,' the old man remarked. 'By your looks, you are not poor and if this Rawat Singh is your friend, he could also not be poor, for friendship can be only among equals. Unless, of course, he has fallen on hard times. But then who can predict the future? Yesterday's Prince can be today's pauper.'

'You're right, Tau.'

Nasrullah had seen enough. Swiftly he came away from the courtyard. In a deserted alley, he removed the trooper's coat and shawl and returned to his apartments. After consuming a light repast, and sending word to his attendants that he was not to be disturbed, he took out his quill, and settled down to compose his report to Murad in his thin, spidery hand.

Your Highness,

Ever since the Emperor became indisposed, I've been

sending reports of His Majesty's medical condition. I am not sure how many of my couriers have reached Ahmedabad after dodging the increasingly tight imperial patrols.

In each of my earlier reports, based on unimpeachable information obtained from people closest to His Majesty—personal access to him continues to remain barred to all except a handful of court officials, and the officially accredited agents of all the Viceroys are under strict surveillance, and their correspondence is monitored—I had stated that his condition was steadily deteriorating, notwithstanding information to the contrary put out by official channels. Indeed, rumours were rife that His Majesty was no more, leading to panic in the bazars, the shutting down of shops and even stray cases of looting.

Now, on the basis of a very reliable source, I gather that three days ago, at the instance of Prince Dara and Jahanara Begum, His Majesty was examined by a Hindu vaid, who is presently camping in Delhi, as a result of whose treatment His Majesty is fast recovering. Indeed it is stated that the figure that appeared at the royal window of audience last morning was the Emperor himself, although some sceptics still maintain that it was actually that of a person made to resemble the Emperor by Prince Dara.

My own assessment is that the Emperor is indeed recovering as a result of this vaid's treatment, who was smuggled into the Emperor's chamber in a burka, and the figure at the window last morning was none other than that of the Emperor. To satisfy myself that this vaid does possess the skills ascribed to him, I went personally and watched him treating patients.

The vaid, who is of very short stature with white hair

and piercing eyes, radiates a confidence and authority that I have seen in few men. He is skilled in the art of medical diagnosis, and his examination of patients is thorough and swift. Patients who had gathered before him this morning were practically unanimous in their opinion that his interventions are unerring, and his treatment is very successful. This I gather from other sources also.

An immediate report will follow if there is any deterioration in the Emperor's medical condition

I remain Your Highness,
Your most obedient servant

After signing it and sprinkling some sand on the paper to dry it, he rolled it and then inserted it into a small cylindrical pouch made of sheep's intestine. He sealed the end with wax, and imprinted his signet ring upon it. If the courier was really cornered, he could always swallow the pouch and would be none the worse, except perhaps for severe indigestion.

He summoned his most able courier Qadir Hussein to his private quarters. Qadir was a gigantic trooper, with a pockmarked, battle-scarred face. His eyes were mere slits and below a fleshy bulbous nose were a pair of thick lips. A puckered streak ran down his left cheek, the result of a sword cut. Although the Mir was a tall man, Qadir Hussein towered over him.

'You sent for me, Master?'

'Yes, Qadir. I have an assignment for you on which the destiny of the empire might well depend. I want you to proceed to Ahmedabad at once and deliver this message to Prince Murad. None else but him, understand?' He held out the pouch to Hussein, who glanced at it and then put it in his inner pocket.

'Word is being sent to the stables to provide you with the swiftest horses, and when you cross the desert, choose the best camels. Expense is of no consequence. Remember, this message must reach Prince Murad in the quickest time possible. If the great Emperor Akbar could perform the journey from Agra to Ahmedabad nearly a hundred years ago with 3,000 troops in eleven days, you should be able to do it in much less time.'

'It shall be done, my Lord,' said the trooper simply.

'Excellent. That is why I have chosen you. Take whoever you want with you but make sure that the message reaches the Prince.'

'I shall travel with two others, my Lord—Imtiaz Ahmed and Munnawar Jamil. I could have travelled alone, but as there is likely to be more than one patrols on the way, it will be advisable if they accompany me. My Lord knows both of them. They are completely trustworthy, and can face any amount of hardship.'

'Which route will you take?'

'We'll go north for some distance, my Lord, to shake off the imperial patrols, and then double back and head for Ajmer; then Jalore, Sirohi, Deesa, Patan and finally Ahmedabad. I have travelled on this very route twice before.'

'Hmmm...Choose whichever route you consider proper. How soon can you leave?

'By sunset.'

That is what Nasrullah Khan liked about Qadir—precision in thought, direct answers, great physical strength, his ability to think on his feet—which made him so invaluable.

'What about funds?'

Qadir said nothing. 'Here take this,' said the Mir, taking a few fistfuls of gold mohurs from a cupboard, placing it in a bag and handing it to the courier. 'If you require more, cash this hundi at the gaddi of Seth Maheshwar Das in Sirohi.' The Mir scribbled few lines on a piece of parchment, signed it and handed it to Qadir. 'He owes me many favours. If you are questioned at the city gate, tell them that you are proceeding to my jagir near Panipat to fetch the head munim along with the rent rolls for my scrutiny, as I have received reports of large-scale embezzlement. If anyone asks you about your mission when you are further afield, tell them that you are going to Ahmedabad to purchase Kathiawari horses for my cavalry regiment. Here is a letter to that effect.'

On another sheet of parchment, the Mir wrote a few lines, folded and sealed it, and then handed the paper to Qadir. 'Now go. Godspeed. Remember, a handsome reward awaits you and your colleagues on the successful accomplishment of this mission.' The Mir went up to the trooper, placed his hands on Qadir's shoulders, looked him straight in the eyes and then said, 'Khuda Hafiz!'

Qadir bowed, turned on his heel and left. He found Ahmed and Jamil playing dice with some others in a verandah of the Mir's palace. He took them aside and said quietly, 'We leave for Ahmedabad by sunset. We have an important message to deliver to Lord Murad. We have to perform the journey at the pace of the wind, travelling by day as well as by night, so that we reach Ahmedabad within five days or at most six, so carry only the essential accoutrements with you. And meet me at the palace stables well before that hour. To anyone who asks, say that we are going to my Lord's jagir near Panipat to fetch the head munim with the revenue registers. We should be away for about two weeks.'

At sunset, Ahmed and Jamil were at the stable door, only

to find Qadir already there, waiting impatiently for them. They were dressed in thick quilted coats and breeches which ended a little below the knee. Their feet were encased in jooties, while around their waist was knotted a sash, from which protruded a dagger. On their head they wore a turban, below which was a light steel skull cap. Each carried a sword, and pistol, along with a round brass studded shield made of tough rhinoceros hide and while Qadir had a bow and a quiver full of arrows slung on his back, the other two carried lances.

After signing out for their mounts and the saddlery, they tightened the girths and then rode out through the busy streets of Delhi. Just as the sun was dipping below the great dome of the Jumma Masjid behind them, they reached the Kashmiri Gate, the northernmost point of entry into the city.

'Where are you heading for?' asked the head gatekeeper as soldiers with crossed lances barred the way.

'We are Lord Nasrullah Khan's men,' replied Qadir. 'We have been sent to my Lord's estates near Panipat to fetch the head munim, with the rent rolls, as embezzlement on a large scale is feared. Would you like to see my Lord's authorization?'

'No need to', replied the gatekeeper. 'If you are going on such an impious task it must be so, although from your accoutrements it would seem that you are more likely going to war, than simply to fetch a munim.'

'One can't be too careful these days,' replied Qadir nonchalantly. 'Only last week an acquaintance of mine was murdered barely half a kos from here. And we don't know what cards this munim might have up his sleeve.'

'Yes, I suppose so. These are indeed uncertain times,' said the gatekeeper as he signalled to a menial and gradually the gate creaked open.

One evening, five days later, the lookouts atop the gate of the fort in Ahmedabad were astonished to see a gigantic trooper and his smaller, rotund companion in the last stages of physical exhaustion, reel groggily out of the saddles of their kneeling camels and fall on the ground in front of the fortress gates. It was Qadir Hussein and Munnawar Jamil. The third trooper, Imtiaz Ahmed, lay recuperating from a grievious knife wound he had sustained during an affray with some of the Nawab of Deesa's men en-route, who had tried to bar their path.

'We are Mir Nasrullah Khan's men from Delhi and we bear a personal message of the utmost importance for Lord Murad,' cried out Qadir to the head gatekeeper as he ran his finger for the umpteenth time around the small pouch that nestled under his shirt. Slowly the heavy gates of the city opened to let them in.

Three

THE LARGE HALL, surrounded on all sides by deep colonnades and situated in the centre of Prince Murad's palace in Ahmedabad, was bathed in the soft lights of the lamps located in different parts of the room and in niches in the walls. A mehfil was in progress and these lights were reflected a thousandfold by the tiny mirrors that glittered in the roof and the supporting pillars. At one end of the hall, seated on matresses covered with white cloth, were the musicians, dressed in their traditional costume of long collarless shirt, chooridar pajamas, coloured velvet waistcoat and embroidered skull cap. They consisted of the tabla player, the sitarist, the pakhawaj player and the person on the harmonium, and in their midst sat the singer, a plump woman with an over-painted face dressed in a green silk sari.

Murad was seated on a divan and was reclining on a bolster with his feet folded up. He was a heavily built man, and his lifestyle of many excesses made him look older than his 33 years. By his side on the divan was a tray containing a long-necked wine flagon with a curved spout, his jade drinking cup and a golden box with separate receptacles for paan, kattha, betel nuts, chunam and opium. At his feet reposed a spitoon.

All around the hall, sprawled or reclining on cushions and blosters, were ranged Murad's courtiers and boon companions.

The singer was rendering a semi-classical khayal composition, and in the centre of the hall the famous Shakeela Bai, dressed in the customary kathak dancer's costume, was coming to the end of her performance.

'Here, Shakeela, take this,' said Murad, as he removed a thick rope of pearls that hung around his neck, and held it tantalizingly before her. The dancer came up coyly to Murad, whose passions were now being slowly aroused. As Shakeela came near, Murad saw her proud, perky breasts straining against her muslin kurta, and the beads of sweat that had formed on her forehead. The scent of the attar she had applied, combined with the perspiration, was something which Murad found intoxicating. He pulled her towards himself and then thrust the necklace between the cleavage of her ample breasts. Delicately, she released herself from Murad's grip, and twirled away in a breathtakingly fluid movement, which took her past the other courtiers.

She came to a stop with arms upraised in the center of the hall and waited for the accompanying musicians to strike the chord, proceeding to hit the floor with the ball of the foot and then with the heel, first with one foot then with the other, and then both feet alternately. As Shakeela continued to perform this movement, she looked up and found that Murad, whose attention span was short, was now beginning to lose interest. He cleared his throat and then spat into the spitoon held up for him by one of the courtiers. Then he clapped his hands.

At the sound of the clap, all present in the hall knew that

the mehfil was over. With a last twirl and a bow, Shakeela edged away from the centre of the hall, and disappeared behind the colonnades. Likewise, the musicians picked up their instruments and rapidly left, followed by the singer. One by one the courtiers got up and left. As the last of them withdrew, Murad's favourite eunuch, Buland, sensing his master's needs, appeared from behind a pillar in the colonnade. He salaamed but seeing that Murad was in his cups, there was a hint of insolence in his eyes.

'Master needs anything?'

'Prepare a woman. The same one we had taken on the hunt to Wankaner last week.'

'Mahajabeen, Sire?'

'Yes, yes, if that's her name. You can't expect us to remember all their names, can you? Get the tall one with the green eyes.'

Buland bowed and went out to execute his master's bidding. He was beside himself with joy, but concealed his happiness as he hustled through the corridors of the palace to the khawaspura, where the concubines were housed. His plan was likely to come to fruition sooner than expected.

For the last one and a half years, he had been having a mortal feud with Ali Naqi, the minister sent by the Emperor from Delhi to straighten out the viceroyalty's finances and give sound counsel to the wayward Murad Baksh. Stern and incorruptible but at the same time highly opinionated, and conscious that he held his brief from the Emperor, Naqi had given short shrift to the sycophants and toadies that surrounded Murad, and in the process had alienated several important nobles. Buland had his eye on a particularly valuable crown property in Rajkot Subah, which Murad had promised to transfer to him at a fraction of its actual value. But Naqi had stoutly opposed the transfer, and Murad had been reluctant to reject openly the advice of his minister who so clearly enjoyed the Emperor's confidence. Similarly Abdul Khesgi, the Faujdar of Patan, too had incurred Naqi's wrath for his high-handedness and extravagance, and both Buland and Khesgi had entered into a conspiracy to strike against Naqi when the time was ripe. An opportunity had presented itself when rumors began to circulate in Ahmedabad that the emperor was at death's door. A letter had been forged over the signature and seal of Ali Naqi by the two conspirators, addressed to Dara, pledging his adherence to the law of primogeniture in the event of the unfortunate demise of the Emperor, and it had been allowed to fall into Murad's hands. The gullible fool had become livid. His anger had ratcheted a few notches higher when the Mir's latest report that the Emperor was recovering through a vaid's treatment, was brought by Qadir Hussein two days earlier.

'Buland, what do you make of this?' Murad had asked, waving the report in front of him.

'Utterly ludicrous, Sire. Absolutely impossible! This fantastic story is clearly a part of the elaborate plot hatched by Prince Dara to lull everyone into complacency by saying that the emperor is on the road to recovery, and at the same time try to win over the Hindu nobility by crediting a vaid for the cure, while he himself consolidates his grip on Delhi. In fact, this humble creature feels that Mir Saheb is playing a double game and has become a pawn in Prince Dara's hands. Clearly Nawab Naqi Saheb is also a part of this conspiracy for otherwise he would not have written that letter pledging allegiance to Prince Dara, knowing His Majesty's precarious medical condition,' replied the wily eunuch.

'Mmmm…I'm beginning to think so too.'

Buland knew that the gunpowder had been stacked against Naqi, and all that was now required was to light the fuse. Mahajabeen would be the instrument for the purpose.

Passing through the innumerable corridors of the palace, Buland reached the khawaspura, which consisted of a series of pavilions and courtyards subdivided by draperies and curtains into cubicles, where Murad's slave girls and concubines resided. Numbering well over a hundred, and drawn from various regions, they ranged from timid, innocent young girls scarcely into their teens captured in the latest raid, to those who had spent the best years of their lives immured behind these high walls and were perhaps remembering that single night when they had been called to Murad's bed, and were hoping against hope that they would be summoned again. All of them had been chosen for their beauty and grace, and they sat there, adorning themselves and playing dice or gossiping, waiting to know whose turn it would be to share Murad's bed that night.

As Murad's favorite eunuch, it was Buland's prerogative to select his master's companion for the night and he knew that he held immense power over these girls. If after a union the concubine happened to conceive, and the infant was fortunate enough to be a boy, then for the mother, the world would open out like a treasure trove. Even though the child would be illegitimate, it would mean immediate elevation in the mother's status, with lands, titles, riches, official preferment and more. If the child was gifted and lucky, he could rise to become a high official of the empire or a great commander. With luck and determination, he could even carve out his own principality, with the mother acquiring the position of the Rajmata. By the same token, some might spend years waiting in vain to be summoned, till they were supplanted by those younger and more beautiful than themselves. It was hardly surprising then that Buland was wooed, beseeched, entreated and feted by these slave girls, for just that single moment with Murad. If rumors were to be believed, even if Buland was unable to consummate a union, it had not prevented him from enjoying the favours of some of the loveliest of the slave girls, in some secluded corner, in return for giving them access to the Viceroy.

As Buland entered the harem, the girls got up and crowded around him, hoping to catch his eye. 'How do I look tonight?' simpered one, as she fluttered her eyelashes and pirouetted before him. 'She looks like the hag she always is,' said another as she pushed the first one aside and thrust herself forward, 'That's why she was returned that night after barely half an hour. Select me, Buland, and I promise His Highness the experience of a lifetime. I shall take him to such pinnacles of pleasure as he has never reached before.'

'Not her, but me,' said yet another, standing in the rear and clapping her hands as she jumped up and down amidst the gaggle of girls to attract Buland's attention. With each jump, clouds of perfume escaped into the air.

'You promised me, Buland, that you would select me tonight,' said a tall willowy girl, in a lime-green gharara and matching choli, her fair rounded arms laden with jewellery.

'Not tonight, girls,' said Buland, as he extricated himself from the melee and went deeper into the harem. 'Perhaps, another time. None of us are going anywhere and there will be plenty of other occasions. Meanwhile, if you want to be chosen again, Bilqees, I would suggest you put on a little less jewellery. You know that His Highness does not like anything to come between him and bare flesh.' Bilqees tore off the bangles and rings she was wearing and flung them aside. Crestfallen at being openly snubbed she burst into tears.

'He'll probably take that slut, Mahajabeen,' said one of Bilqees' friends spitefully. 'Honestly I don't know what His Highness sees in that bitch. She looks cold as ice and quite frankly those eyes of hers, they frighten me.'

Although still within earshot, Buland pretended he hadn't heard these remarks. In any case, he was used to such malicious and venomous comments from these concubines, who had nothing to engage their minds and were forever backbiting. Proceeding further, he passed through several pavilions and at length spotted her. She was sitting under the starlight on a low parapet that enclosed a fountain, and was trailing her fingers idly in the water, watching the goldfish dart in and out amidst the ornamental stones on the floor of the fountain.

'Ah! There you are Mahajabeen!' he said.

At the sound of her name being called out, the seventeen-year-old girl stood up. She was a Circassian beauty, who had been captured by the Faujdar of Surankot in a raid and sent to Murad, as token of his fealty. Tall for a girl, Mahajabeen had a milk-white complexion, and thick glossy black hair, long enough for her to sit on. Her widely spaced green eyes steadily looked at the world, beneath delicately arched eyebrows. Her soft peach-like cheeks had gorgeous dimples, and behind a full ruby-red mouth lay a set of perfect teeth. The beauty of her face was matched by the symmetry of her body, for her pert bosom tapered down to a narrow waist which could be encircled by two hands, and flared into generous hips. The legs in their white muslin chooridar pajamas were long and shapely.

'Yes, Buland?' Mahajabeen's voice was soft and musical.

'Come, child. His Highness has asked specially for you. It

is a rare honour. I can remember only one other case when he asked for the same girl twice within the space of ten days. We must hurry. You know he doesn't like to be kept waiting. Luckily, you do not require any cosmetics at all.'

He shepherded her to her cubicle where two waiting slave girls helped her to disrobe. Then, she stepped delicately into the adjacent hammam and was bathed in rose water.

As Buland sat on a stool in the hammam, watching Mahajabeen being readied, in all his years, he could not recall a girl as good-looking as her. Not only was she beautiful, but Buland had noticed that she possessed a lively intelligence as well. With the utmost care he had groomed her. He had supervised her diet so that her breath smelt sweet and wholesome at all times and he had even lain with her at night over an extended period to ensure that no foul smell emanated from her. Her facial and body hair had been removed and various rare oils and unguents had been rubbed into her skin, to make it soft and yielding. Buland had paid attention to her deportment and behaviour as well. She was taught how to hold Murad's interest, how to make polite conversation, along with the more mundane things such as how to fold and offer a paan, and how to pour wine from a flagon. Although Murad had professional singers to entertain him, Mahajabeen was also coached in the fundamentals of Hindustani music. Above all Buland had initiated her into the mysteries of womanhood and how to use her charms so as to give Murad pleasure, so that he would want her again and again.

When Buland felt that Mahajabeen was ready, he had waited for a suitable occasion to present her to Murad. That occasion came when the Viceroy drew up a programme for a week-long lion hunt in Wankaner. Normally on such occasions, he took two or three concubines with him, but Buland had persuaded him to take Mahajabeen alone, and it seemed that Buland's persuasion had paid off. On her return from Wankaner, Mahajabeen had recounted how physically painful the loss of her virginity had been, but she had put all her lessons to good use, and soon had Murad eating out of her hand. He had showered her with costly presents, and on the last night of the hunt, he had even offered to make her one of his junior wives.

Buland did not attach any credence to this, but he knew that Murad would ask for Mahajabeen again, and that he could use her to attack Naqi. In the long glistening hours of the afternoon, he had coached her how to veer the conversation with Murad towards gossip in the harem, and in the process insinuate that the real ruler of Gujarat was not Murad but Ali Naqi. Fully aware of Murad's egotistical and volcanic temper, Buland knew that added to the other material built up against Ali Naqi, it would be sufficient for the Viceroy to react violently against the minister.

As Mahajabeen stepped out of the hammam a light perfume was sprayed all over her body, special attention being paid to the pulse points—the area behind the earlobes and between the thighs. Buland had chosen for her a pure white muslin backless long-sleeved choli and gharara, which set of her glorious complexion, and while looking prim, revealed all the rich contours of her body with an understated elegance. The only piece of jewellery she had on was a diamond star-burst necklace tied with a black ribbon tightly around her neck. Her hair was left loose and flowing under a white odhni.

Then, lest she perspire on the way, she was made to sit in a small golden cart encrusted with gems, which was pulled with silken ropes by two slave girls, with Buland accompanying them, to the hall where Murad lay waiting.

'Remember all that I've told you, and God be with you, my child,' whispered the eunuch, as they neared the hall. Meanwhile at his insistence, Murad had been carried to a smaller, more intimate ante chamber adjacent to the hall.

Buland entered the antechamber and announced, 'Mahajabeen is here, Sire. She awaits your pleasure.'

Murad lay sprawled on the divan, one leg hanging over its side. He was breathing heavily and his eyes were closed. The flagon of wine lay empty beside him, his drinking cup was upturned and most of the opium in the paan box had also been consumed. Murad stirred at the announcement and waved Buland away. Buland ushered in Mahajabeen and left. She stood before Murad demurely, who attempted to sit up. He blinked once or twice, shook his head to clear it, but then threw his head back against the bolster and closed his eyes.

Mahajabeen was facing a dilemma. For her own well-being if not to repay her gratitude to Buland, it was vital that she carried Murad's seed within her, as quickly as possible, but to do that the Viceroy had first to be pulled out of his drunken stupor.

'Sire! Wake up, Sire!' she said as she sat down on the edge of the divan and cradled Murad's head in her arms. Murad was showing some signs of movement. His eyes fluttered open for a brief second, and then they closed again, as he snuggled his head in her lap.

Letting his head rest on the bolster, she rose and hastened into the corridor. She saw a slave girl and said, 'Quickly fetch a bowl of water. His Highness is slightly indisposed.'

The girl fled to bring the water. Mahajabeen returned to

the antechamber. Murad was still comatose. As Mahajabeen sat by Murad's side gently wiping his face with her odhni, the girl returned with a bowl full of water. Throwing a grateful glance at her, Mahajabeen took Murad's head in her lap, and then dipping the end of the odhni into the water, she gently wiped his face with it.

Gradually Murad began to stir. 'Mmmmm…that's nice,' he murmured. 'We could lie here for ever. Go on. Continue to do that.'

Suddenly he heard the soft tinkle of Mahajabeen's laughter, like some silver bell heard from afar. He opened his eyes and looked up into Mahajabeen's calm green eyes and her lovely face. 'Sire, I'm afraid I'll have to disturb you. My leg has gone to sleep.'

By this time Murad was fully awake. He pulled himself onto the divan, sat up and peered at his beautiful companion with bloodshot eyes, trying to bring her features into focus.

'What is your name, beautiful one?' he asked at length.

'Mahajabeen, Sire,' said the girl in a voice that was scarcely above a whisper.

'Ah, yes. Now we remember. We had taken you with us on the lion hunt to that place, what's its name? Wanka… something.'

'Wankaner, Sire.'

'Yes, Wankaner. That was a good hunt. We got three lions, and besides that we had you for company. We had asked Buland to send us the girl with the green eyes. That's how we remember you. The girl with the green eyes.' His slack mouth creased into a smile. 'What's your name, did you say?'

Mahajabeen repeated her name.

'The name does justice to the face. Come, sit by our side.

Do not be afraid.' He watched with delight as the girl sat demurely at a corner of the divan, eyes lowered, legs folded at the knees, squeezing the last few drops of water from the end of her odhni with her hand.

He pressed her against the bolster and then planted a searing kiss on her lips.

Mahajabeen recoiled slightly at first, but then quickly she realized that this was no time to be sqeamish. As Murad's lips pressed down on her mouth she parted her lips slightly, which excited him even further. Knitting the fingers of both his hands behind her head, he crushed her face against his, as he rained kisses on her. 'You're so beautiful, so very beautiful,' he murmured against her mouth, as his senses swam.

Mahajabeen was a girl of healthy appetite and she too was getting aroused. 'Take me, take me, Sire,' she whispered, cradling Murad's head against her. 'I don't think I can wait much longer.'

Murad, for all his faults, was a considerate lover. He knew that Mahajabeen, despite the week in Wankaner, was still largely inexperienced and was unaware of the delights her own body was capable of. He was therefore in no hurry and wanted to draw out the love-play as long as possible, but soon his passions overrode his restraint and at length he ground into her in one delirious spasm of ecstasy just as she reached her own climax.

It was the girl's eyes that opened first, well before dawn. It took an instant for Mahajabeen to get her bearings and then with a smile she remembered the events of the previous night. Then she recalled what Buland had required her to do. But how was the subject to be broached?

She saw Murad stirring. He opened his eyes and turned

towards her, drawing her close to him. 'That was a wonderful night. You're the reigning Empress of our heart. Truly, few women have given us so much pleasure as you have. Ask what you want, and you shall have it.'

'Anything, Sire?'

'Yes, if it is anything within reason, of course.'

'There is one thing, Sire. As I said I have taken birth to give you pleasure and there is one thing that you can give me in return, which is entirely within your power to give, and is also entirely reasonable.'

'You shall have it this instant. What is that?'

'Sire, for my sake, take back Gujarat.'

'Take back Gujarat? You speak in riddles, girl. How can we take back what we already have, and what do you mean when you say that for your sake we should take back Gujarat?' asked Murad, looking perplexed. 'We can understand jewels, gold, horses, camels, slave girls as gifts, but Gujarat?'

'The things you mention, Sire, are mere trifles, compared with what you can actually be the master of, provided you take full control of the Subah.'

'Who says we are not in full control? What sort of nonsense is being talked about in the harem? Who has been feeding you with all this rubbish? Tell us, and we will personally have him flayed alive this instant.' By now Murad's temper had been ignited and it was smouldering, as he sat up on the divan.

'Sire, I'm only a little being in the harem and there are many who are senior to me. Moreover I have come only recently, but there is general talk there, that while Your Highness reigns over Gujarat, he does not rule. Instead, it is my Lord Ali Naqi who is the ultimate dispenser, as he has the Emperor's ear. We're inferior beings, Sire, and our brains are not capable of understanding high matters of state but this is the talk I heard within the harem, and as Your Highness has been so kind to me, I've taken courage to bring it to Your Lordship's attention.'

Mahajabeen delicately thrust her body towards Murad, but now he seemed to have lost interest in her physical attractions. He was more intent on knowing what was being said about him in the harem, and he was getting angrier by the minute. *That bastard, Ali Naqi,* he thought. *Always coming in our way and threatening to report matters to the Emperor, if his view did not prevail. So many proposals or rewards to some favourite had been turned down by him on one flimsy pretext or another, and whenever we had tried to insist, we were told that it would require the Emperor's specific approval, knowing full well that it would never come. Are we not Murad, Viceroy of Gujarat, and son of the mightiest Emperor on earth? And yet whatever we wanted to do could be thwarted by a mere minister, a paid functionary of the state. So much so that at times we were treated no better than an errant schoolboy. What was even more galling was that this had now become even the topic of harem gossip, and if this was the state of affairs inside the harem, what must the talk in the bazars be like? Everybody must be laughing behind our back, as being someone whose writ did not run beyond his nose. To cap it all, now that the Emperor was gravely ill and perhaps even on his deathbed, this old rogue was intriguing with that apostate Dara. By God, something had to be done to rid ourself of the thorn in our flesh. With the Emperor irretrievably weakened there was no better time to do so than now.*

The smouldering anger in Murad's breast burst into white-hot flames. He clapped his hands. A slave girl appeared, still rubbing her eyes. 'Bring Buland to us at once. If he is not here within a quarter of this watch, neither you nor he will see the sunset this evening.' The girl hastened to search for the eunuch and bring him before Murad. Then turning to Mahajabeen he said curtly, 'Get dressed. You will see how a scion of the Mughal empire rules.'

In a short time, Buland was in Murad's antechamber. 'You sent for me, Sire?'

'Yes. Where is that letter written by Ali Naqi to our brother Lord Dara?'

'I have it here, Sire.' Buland rummaged within his robe and then fished out the letter. He always kept it with him, knowing that Murad may call for it at any instant. He handed it to Murad reverentially, who opened it and ran his eye over the words for the umpteenth time. His mind was now made up. 'Ask Ali Naqi to appear before us immediately, and if he does not come, drag him here. We shall be sitting out in the adjoining garden,' he said grimly.

When Mahajabeen tried to follow him out into the garden, Murad gently restrained her. 'No, beautiful one. When a Viceroy discusses matters of state with a high minister, they require privacy.'

'Of course, Sire. How thoughtless of me. Forgive me for taking the liberty of daring to think that I could intrude,' she said. She assumed that Murad would give the minister a severe dressing-down. She did not see him take a spear from the guard on duty at the entrance to the garden.

Dawn was breaking over Ahmedabad, as Buland's mesengers reached Ali Naqi's residence to inform him that he had been urgently summoned by Murad. The tall, thin minister with snow-white hair cascading down to his shoulders, bushy eyebrows and beard to match, was reading the Holy Koran when the message was conveyed to him. After completing his prayers, he donned his court dress and proceeded at once into Murad's presence and found him seated in a chair in the garden, with both feet raised, holding the spear in his left hand. He looked unkempt in his crushed kurta and pajamas, with hair uncombed.

'Ah! Welcome Naqi Saheb,' began Murad sarcastically. 'It's good to see you so early in the morning. We were informed that normally you do not rise before noon.'

'Sire, I am here because Your Highness' messengers came to summon me. As for my not rising before noon, whoever has told Your Highness that has blatantly lied because whether it is deep winter or high summer, I am at my beads well before dawn and deal with state papers immediately thereafter. In any case, surely Your Highness did not send for me at this hour to inquire about my daily routine?'

'Indeed, we did. In fact, we are curious to know whether it is during the day or the night that you think up all those ingenious objections, whenever we desire to recognize someone for his loyalty or reward somebody for his good work.' Murad's voice was dangerously menacing.

'Your Highness is aware that I have strongly supported all those cases where the display of loyalty has been genuine, and the work has been demonstrably good. I have gone out of my way to recommend such cases to Your Highness.'

'So, you consider yourself the best judge of loyalty and good work, do you?'

'I never said that, Your Highness. But even a child would know that a eunuch, who panders to someone's basest passions and continually misleads for private gain, cannot be said to display loyalty, and a Faujdar who rack rents his tenants to build yet another palace when the most appalling famine is stalking his territories and people under his charge are dying like flies, can scarcely be credited with doing good work.' The reference to Buland and Khesgi, who happened to be another of Murad's favourites, was obvious, and each word, uttered deliberately at a measured pace, struck across Murad's face like a lash.

'Have a care. Have a care, Ali Naqi,' said Murad, his voice practically choking with rage. 'Even if you happen to have been sent here by the Emperor, do not forget that you are standing before the Emperor's son.' His grip tightened on the spear in his hand.

'Your Highness has never let me forget it,' replied the aged minister mildly. 'Now Your Highness must excuse me. There are certain urgent matters to be attended to, and you may send for me when you are in a suitable frame of mind for purposeful discussion.' Naqi turned on his heel and was ready to walk away.

'Stop! How dare you show your back to us and walk away when we have not finished with you? Don't you know before whom you are standing?'

The minister stopped, turned back and looked pityingly at Murad. 'As I mentioned, Your Highness, I've not been allowed to forget it for a moment. Now, Your Highness must tell me what use I can be to you at this hour. Otherwise, as there is a lot of pending work, permit me to go and attend to it. Your Highness can send for me later in the day at your convenience.'

Meanwhile, Mahajabeen had lain down on the divan to catch a little sleep after Murad had left to speak to the minister. The night's hectic lovemaking had caused a pleasant ache in her limbs and her last thoughts before she fell into slumber were of Murad entering her. She woke up with a start, to find Buland with his face glued to the lattice, which commanded a view of the garden.

'What's happening?' she asked.

'Nothing,' Buland replied, not taking his eyes off from the events in the garden. 'Ali Naqi has been sent for by His Highness, and it appears that he is being given a good verbal thrashing. Serves that old fool right.' Mahajabeen could not miss the triumph in Buland's voice.

She got up from the divan and stood next to Buland, watching the altercation between the Emperor's son and the old minister. Although they were too far away to hear what was being said, she saw Ali Naqi turning and walking away, Murad sitting up in his chair and shouting something, and Naqi turning back to face him again.

'I fear for the old man,' she whispered to Buland, her face pressed against the lattice. 'Did you see the way His Highness' grip tightened over the spear? Don't you think we should do something?' There was concern in her voice for she felt that she was responsible for bringing Ali Naqi into this situation, a man she had never seen before and now that she had seen him, a man who looked older than her grandfather.

'Ssshhh child...there's nothing that we can do,' said Buland, his nose glued to the lattice. 'How can we interfere in a matter between the Emperor's son and his minister? In any case, nothing is going to happen. His Highness seems too exhausted to be able to do anything. Kept him up all night, did you? How many times?' he passed his hand round Mahajabeen's waist, gave her soft breast a squeeze and smiled wickedly.

Mahajabeen removed Buland's arm, and kept looking at the garden. She felt a sickening sense of foreboding.

Murad was getting impatient. 'No. Now that you are here, we might as well get it over with. What in your lexicon is the punishment for treason?'

'Why, death of course,' replied the minister.

'Are you absolutely sure? Think well before answering.'

'Yes, I have no doubt of it. Treason is a capital offence. So say our schools of legal thought. It shakes the very foundations of society and makes it prey to external invasion and internal chaos.'

'Then how do you explain this letter to our brother, Dara?' roared Murad, as he whipped out the letter and threw it at Naqi's face. 'There is no confirmation that the Emperor is no more, and here you are, already pledging your allegiance to our brother, although the mandate given to you was to serve us and give us good counsel here in Gujarat. Is that not treason?'

For an instant, the great minister was perplexed. What was this drug-crazed fool talking about? What letter was this? He picked up the letter that had fallen at his feet and read it. A smile of triumph creased his weary face. 'If people want to forge my signature, they could at least do a better job of it. See the letter "nun" in my name Naqi, which is said to have been signed by me. The dot should be above the point where the curve begins, but in this case it is practically in the center of the curve. This is an outright forgery, and a crude one at that. My calligraphy has been praised even by His Majesty, and surely you don't think that I would write in so slovenly a manner, do you?'

'And what about this preposterous story that is being fed to us, by a person whom we trusted, that the Emperor was recovering though treatment of his illness by a Hindu vaid? You're also associated with this canard, at the instance of our brother Dara, whose sympathies are well known to be with people of that faith, are you not?'

'I've no idea what you're talking about,' replied Ali Naqi

indignantly. 'The world knows that His Majesty has been indisposed and it is natural for him to receive treatment, but from a Hindu Vaid? Why, are the palace physicians not competent enough?'

'You tell us. Is not this a conspiracy hatched by our brother Dara to win over the support of the Hindu nobility, in the event of a struggle for succession, in which you too are actively involved?'

The minister leaned on his stick and looked steadily at Murad seated on the chair. Then his voice rang out. 'Allow me to speak bluntly, Your Highness. For forty years, I have served the empire faithfully. From the snowy wastes of Kandahar to the jungles of Bengal, wherever I have been sent, my services have been appreciated. The only ones who have rejoiced at my departure have been the rogues, the scoundrels and the sycophants. It is to clean up the mess in this viceroyalty that His Majesty had sent me here, and as a loyal servant of the Emperor, I obeyed. On coming here, I found Your Highness surrounded by sycophants, flatterers and scoundrels of the worst kind who have been bleeding the Subah dry for their own gain. I have tried more than once to advise Your Highness to be on your guard against them, but instead of recognizing who your real foes are, you have chosen to believe them instead of me. Now on the basis of their machinations, which you haven't seen through, I am being accused of treason on the strength of a crass forgery. I am also accused of being involved in spreading falsehood, to influence a certain faction in a possible war of succession in the event of the emperor's unfortunate demise, even when the Emperor lives. Indeed Your Highness, such thought itself is treason, and I shall not be a part of it.'

By now the minister was quivering with emotion, and

he uttered the last few sentences, shaking his stick at Murad. Behind the lattice, Mahajabeen watched with increasing horror what was transpiring in the garden. When she saw Ali Naqi raising his stick, and Murad stand up, his face contorted with rage, she knew something dreadful was about to happen. She saw Murad grip the spear in his hands and point it at the minister. 'Oh, my God, he's going to kill the old man,' she cried, as she tore herself from the lattice and tried to run to the aid of the minister. Buland, however, was too quick for her. As she turned, he spun around and held her by the waist and pressing her head against his shoulder, his hand covered her eyes.

'No child, it is not for us to interfere in such matters,' he said.

He heard Murad scream, 'Miserable wretch! Eating the salt of our viceroyalty, and yet turn traitor, would you?' Buland's eyes gleamed with triumph as he watched Murad thrust the spear into Ali Naqi's body. The spear pierced Ali Naqi in the abdomen. With a great groan, he fell to the ground. At that instant Buland found that Mahajabeen had become limp in his arms.

Murad clapped his hands. Some gardeners and aides who were watching the events from the far end of the garden made a terrified appearance. 'Have this carcass removed,' Murad commanded, pointing with his foot to the minister's body lying before him, eyes and mouth open. 'See that his bloodstains do not soil the grass.'

Four

FAR TO THE east, some days' march from the provincial capital of Dhaka, Prince Shuja Shukoh, second son of the Emperor, and Viceroy of Bengal, was in the midst of a great hunt. For nearly a week now, hundreds of beaters had been labouring to drive the game in ever-narrowing concentric circles into a compact arena. Now, under the afternoon sun, Shuja and several other members of the nobility, seated on elephants, were waiting in a clearing in the bowl of a shallow valley whose slopes were heavily forested with sal and sheesham trees and grass as tall as a man's height for the beaters to drive the animals towards them.

Seated on the largest elephant was Shuja himself, a tall imposing figure, with a central Asian cast of features, characterized by his narrow eyes and long, thin face sparsely covered with a beard and moustache. By his side sat his son Zain-ul- Abidin, a slender, handsome young lad of fourteen who was being taken on his first great tiger hunt. Behind them were Tugrhil Mian, the head huntsman, and two gun loaders, with an assortment of weapons for the hunt, while seated in front was the mahout. On either side of Shuja, also mounted on elephants, and spaced out at a distance of a few paces from each other in a rough semicircle were several other dignitaries of his court, including his Chief Wazir, the Vakil and his Master General of Ordnance.

'When will these animals come?' asked Zain in a bored voice. Beads of perspiration had formed on his smooth forehead and were beginning to run down his cheek. Shuja pulled out a handkerchief from his sleeve and tenderly wiped the boy's face with it. The sun blazed bright and hot, and the beautifully tasseled umbrella fastened to the howdah offered little protection from its fierce rays.

'Just a little while longer,' said Shuja. 'See, the beaters have to do a big job. They have to drive all the animals and birds before them and it will take a little while longer for them to reach us.'

'We have been sitting here for the last two watches, and haven't even seen a chicken,' said the boy plaintively. 'At this rate, we wonder whether any game will come our way at all.'

'Don't worry. Game is plentiful in these parts, and you shall have the honor of shooting your first Royal Bengal tiger,' said Shuja.

'How wonderful that will be,' exclaimed Miandad. 'We shall have the tiger skinned, and then it will be mounted opposite your own tiger skin in your private apartments.'

Shuja laughed heartily. He doted on the boy, and of all his sons, saw much of himself in him. In his more expansive moments, Shuja mused that after himself it would be Zain who would rule the empire. After all, how long had the emperor to live? Already there were reports that he was gravely ill. After he passed on, the empire would be Shuja's, and Shuja's alone. In any case, Dara was too weak to wield the sceptre, and Murad had not the least idea what was going on. Yes, Aurangzeb might pose a problem, but there were ways of neutralizing him too. After all, was not he, Shuja, Subahdar of Bengal, the richest viceroyalty in the empire? Its gold was enough to buy up all those who might think of supporting Aurangzeb, who could then be pensioned off, or perhaps induced to undertake a Haj. Had not Akbar sent Bairam Khan on just such a pilgrimage before grasping the reins of power? In fact, all three brothers could be induced to undertake that pilgrimage. Many things could happen on the journey. Till then of course he must bide his time.

'I see birds, Sire,' said Tughril Mian, pointing towards a flock of egrets that were winging their way towards the hunting party.

'You're right, Tughril,' said Shuja, scanning the sky, using his hand to shade his eyes. 'Although we can't hear the beaters as yet, they should not be very far off. How much time do you give the animals, particularly the bigger and faster ones, to reach us?'

'About half a watch, Sire,' replied Tughril. He was a wrinkled little man with one eye and practically no nose. He had been mauled by a tiger as a boy during one of Akbar's last great hunts. Miraculously he had survived, and had served Jahangir and later Shah Jahan, before he had been picked up by Shuja for his peerless tracking skills.

'Are all the muskets primed? We hope you have brought our favorite Jaanbaaz with you,' said Shuja.

'Yes, Sire. All the guns are ready, and Jaanbaaz is here.' Tughril nodded towards a beautifully fashioned matchlock that stood propped up along with others in a corner of the howdah.

'Give it to Nawabzada Saheb here. He should have no difficulty in bagging his first tiger with it,' said Shuja.

Tughril took the firearm and handed it to Zain. The boy lifted it to his shoulder, and then swung it in the air, as if he were taking a flying shot and then aimed at the stump of a tree in the distance. Looking satisfied with the firearm, he handed it back to Tughril.

'Excellent!' remarked Shuja. 'You have the feel of the weapon already. This will be your baptism as a great shikari.'

The flight of birds had steadily increased, indicating that there was some disturbance in the forest. The restlessness of the birds affected the elephants too. The one next to Shuja, on which his Chief Wazir Bismillah Khan was seated with his gun bearers, suddenly swerved and its rump collided with the side of Shuja's own elephant. One of the loaders, who was placing the musket Jaanbaaz in its position along with the other muskets, was pushed against an ivory knob of the howdah, which hit him in the nose. There was a grating sound of cartilage tearing as the man stood up screaming in agony, nursing his bleeding nose.

'Stupid oaf,' shouted Shuja at the unfortunate man. 'Are you going to ruin the entire hunt? Send this man back to the camp. Which idiot brought him along? Tughril, was it you?'

'No, Sire, I am not to blame. In fact the regular loader was suddenly taken ill and I was told by the shikars that this man would be a reliable substitute,' murmured Tughril, mortally afraid to offend his master. Then with the assistance of the other loader, Tughril helped the injured man out of the howdah, and over the elephant's rear on to the ground, from where he ran back to the camp.

Among the dozen or so elephants that stood in the clearing there was now expectation that something was about to happen. Overhead the sky was dotted with birds who were seeking to escape from the disturbance to their habitat on the ground, while the sweep of the beaters was so wide that the creatures within their net had no recourse except to pour down the sides of the valley towards the hunting party.

Suddenly Tughril cocked his ear. 'The beaters are approaching, Sire,' he said quietly. 'I hear the sound of crackers.' He strained his ear towards the approaching sound. 'The advance line of beaters is not more than one kos away. We should expect the first of the animals trying to break cover very soon now.'

'Pass the word on both sides then, to be alert,' said Shuja.

The sound of the approaching beaters was now getting louder. A low roar could be heard in the distance accompanied by the staccato beat of drums, the clash of cymbals and the clank of pots and pans, interspersed with the cries of loud voices, 'Huh, huh, huh, huh, dreeeaahhh, huk, huk…'

The first to break cover was a magnificent neelgai. It stuck its head through the tall grass and sniffed the air. As the hunting party stood in its lee, it could not pick up their scent. Meanwhile, the pressure being built up by the animals in its rear was increasing. Believing it had nothing to fear, the neelgai edged forward.

Shuja had let it be known that he and his son Zain were not interested in shooting anything but a tiger, and as he and the boy sat watching, the Chief Wazir Bismillah Khan was given the honour of opening the hunt. As the neelgai emerged from the grass cover, Shuja shouted, 'The beast is yours, Bismillah Saheb.'

Bismillah stood up in his howdah. Placing the stock of the musket against his chin, he took aim and fired, but the neelgai was too quick. It had seen the barrel glinting in the sun, and just as Bismillah fired, it swerved and the bullet hit only its hind leg. But not for nothing was Tughril renowned as one of the keenest shots in the empire. Standing behind Shuja, with a loaded musket, its stock at his chin, he was prepared for just such an eventuality. As the wounded animal tried to hobble back into the grass Tughril fired at it, piercing its skull.

'Well done, Tughril,' exclaimed Shuja, as two of Bismillah's gun bearers leapt over the side of the elephant and raced to the mortally wounded animal. One of them whipped out his knife and ran the blade over the beast's epiglottis, which was soon a wide gaping wound, through which blood was pouring out. Even as the deer was in its last death agonies, the two gun bearers caught it by its hind legs and dragged it along the ground to a side of the clearing.

The tide of animals coming towards the hunting party steadily increased. Sambhar, neelgai, antelope, gazelles, bison and hogs tried to flee from the beaters who were advancing relentlessly upon them from the rear, forcing them on to the hunting party. Soon the noise made by the beaters had become a dull insistent roar, broken by the bursting of crackers, and amidst those noises could be heard occasionally the terrified cry of some animal. As the trickle of animals kept increasing, some nobles seated on the elephants dismounted, forsaking their muskets or bow to try their skill with sword and lance. Soon the clearing had become a huge charnel house with the elephants turning, wheeling and swerving, while around them the animals lay dead or dying as they tried to break the iron ring of the huntsmen.

Suddenly there was the sound of some heavy animal rustling in the undergrowth. 'Be ready, Sire. It's a tiger.' murmured Tughril.

'Are you ready, Zain?' asked Shuja, in a hoarse whisper. The boy nodded. He had been handed the loaded Jaanbaaz, and as its stock snuggled against his cheek, the barrel resting against the side of the howdah, he waited for the tiger to emerge from the grass.

Tughril was not wrong. A huge tiger thrust its head cautiously through the cover of the grass, and seemed perplexed about his escape route.

Meanwhile the elephants had become aware that a tiger was in their midst. An instinctive fear gripped the elephant immediately to Shuja's right, and that fear was transmitted to one or two others. Shuja's own elephant began pawing the ground restlessly, and shifting its position, as it lifted its trunk and trumpeted loudly. 'Keep the animal still!' commanded Shuja, afraid that the elephant's movement would spoil Zain's shot, but the sudden passage of a couple of warthogs in the space between the elephants only made them more restless. Terrified by the noise and alarmed by the presence of the tiger in their close vicinity, the hogs had broken cover and dashed through the clearing, zig-zagging between the hunters on the ground on the one hand, and Shuja's elephant and the one immediately to his right, on the other. Mistaking the animal near its feet to be the tiger, Shuja's elephant side stepped vigorously and at that very instant, the tiger decided to make a break for it. As the tiger bounded forward, seeking a gap between the elephants, Zain fired, but the unstable motion of the elephant made the ball go awry. One or two of the shikaris on the ground tried vainly to stab at the tiger with their swords as it flashed past, but they were horribly mauled in the process, and the powerfully muscled beast, finding a gap between them, was able to gain the cover of the grass on the opposite side.

'You son of a whore,' shouted Shuja, livid with rage at the miserable little mahout for failing to keep the elephant still. 'Which idiot made you a mahout? We shall teach you a lesson that you will not forget. Throw this man down and tie him up.'

'Have pity on this unfortunate creature, Master,' cried the mahout. 'Have pity on me. What will become of my wife and children?'

'Wretch! Rascal! It is people like you who bring more idiots into the world.'

Shuja brutally pushed the mahout to the ground. The two loaders swiftly descended, trussed up the unfortunate mahout and then looked up to Shuja for further orders. Shuja snatched a loaded musket lying at the back of the howdah, aimed at the mahout's waist and fired. The bullet tore through the man's hip, leaving him writhing in agony, unable to move. Just then a wild buffalo succeeded in reaching up to the elephants. The poor mahout lay directly in his path, and amidst a flurry of slashing hooves and flailing horns, his dying screams were carried far into the surrounding forest, till the buffalo was brought down by a well-aimed shot and collapsed in the midst of the mahout's bleeding entrails.

Even Tughril, who had seen enough cruelty in his lifetime, was sickened at the sight of the innocent mahout's body lying broken and trampled upon, but he dared not say anything.

'Now get a better mahout than that one,' said Shuja to Tughril.

Zain had been watching all this silently. Baulked of the prize of slaying a royal Bengal tiger, sulkily he rolled a ball of spittle in his mouth and then spat it accurately at the dead mahout.

For Shuja also, the loss of the tiger had made the hunt lose its savour. He abruptly called it off, and as the sun was setting the cavalcade of elephants with the immense retinue of shikaris and attendants wended its way back to camp.

As Shuja was resting in his tent along with Zain and drinking wine, an attendant came to the tent flap and said that Tughril begged to be received.

'Very well, send him in,' replied Shuja. Tughril stood before Shuja, barely able to contain his excitement.

'Sire, I am told by the local villagers that there is a water course, not far from here, where wild animals come regularly to drink, and I have no doubt that if we build a machan there, we should be able to bag a tiger this night itself. If Nawabzada Saheb would care to sit up tonight, I can assure him that a tiger will be his,' said Tughril.

'Oh yes, we would love that,' said Zain excitedly.

'An excellent idea! Have the machan constructed at once. We shall sit up for the tiger this night. What was the afternoon's bag?'

'Twelve neelgais, two wild buffaloes, thirty-seven sambhars, eight warthogs forty-one gazelles and innumerable smaller animals.'

'It's a pity that the tiger escaped us. Had that wretched mahout not lost control of the elephant, we would have given you the title of Sher Khan by now, Zain. However it's still not too late. If what Tughril says is true, the title shall yet be yours before the sun rises tomorrow.' Then turning to Tughril, Shuja said, 'To make doubly sure that the tiger makes an appearance, why not also tie a bait?'

'A bait near a waterhole, Sire?' Tughril could not conceal the doubt in his voice.

'Hunger or thirst. What has impelled animals since the

dawn of time? One or the other, or maybe both.'

'Very well, Sire,' Tughril agreed quickly, as he knew it was dangerous to argue with Shuja.

'And let it not be some ordinary bait, like a goat or buffalo, let it be live human bait.'

'Human bait, Sire? But what if one of us misses?' Tughril was alarmed by such an idea.

'Enough. We have decided that it shall be human bait and so it shall be. To make sure that the human being is not aware what is happening, let an infant be brought and given a sleeping draught. Now Tughril, send someone to one of the nearby villages to procure an infant. Tell the family members that they will be well compensated.'

A dastarkhwan had been spread in the royal tent and there Shuja and Zain ate a meal of biryani and partridge curry, washed down with wine.As they were completing their meal, Shuja heard the wailing of a woman not very far from the tent. A few seconds later, the flap of the tent parted and an attendant stood respectfully outside, head bowed.

'We have procured the infant, Sire, but the parents are inconsolable and beseech Your Highness that they be used as bait instead.'

Shuja stepped out of the tent. He saw a young woman, wailing loudly, with tears streaming down her cheeks. She was beating her breasts, and her sari was all undone, with her hair straggling all across her face. Along with her was a young man, obviously her husband, looking equally distraught.

'Take me as bait, Master,' the woman wailed, pointing a shaking hand towards an infant that lay asleep in the arms of one of the accompanying attendants. 'What has this little mite done to annoy one so great as yourself? See, my flesh will be far more appetizing for the tiger than this little creature. Have pity on it.'

The child's father added his own entreaties to his wife's tearful pleas but to no avail. 'Be silent, woman,' retorted Shuja. 'Nothing will happen to your child. We have never been known to miss our prey, and Tughril here has shot over a hundred tigers. We give you our word that no harm will befall your child. Here, take this.' Shuja reached for his waistband and drew out a bag containing gold coins. He threw the bag at the mother. She opened the bag. It contained more money than she had seen in her entire lifetime. She grabbed the bag. 'You will be careful, will you not, Sire?' she said between her sobs. 'You will return him safe and sound to us, will you not?'

'Yes, yes. Now be off. Your child will be returned to you safe and sound, tomorrow morning,' said Shuja.

The attendants led the woman and her husband away, as one of them cradled the infant.

A machan was quickly constructed in a large simhal tree that commanded an unrivalled view of the watercourse. When all was ready, riding horses were brought to cover the distance and Tughril led the way, followed by some lancers, and then Shuja and Zain. A few guards brought up the rear, one of whom carried the infant, who by now lay fast asleep dozed with opium. As Shuja, Zain and Tughril settled themselves in the machan, the infant, naked save for an amulet tied around its waist, was placed in a small depression near the lip of the watercourse.

All three now waited for the tiger to appear.

It was a moonlit night, which made the waters look like burnished silver. There was pin-drop silence all around except for the occasional croak of frogs and the 'cheep-cheep' of crickets. Fireflies were dancing in the undergrowth, chasing each other in a bizzarre display of acrobatics. Suddenly there was the raucous cry of some animal. Slowly and carefully a tiger emerged from the thick vegetation that lined the water course and surveyed the scene. It could get the scent of the infant lying in front of him near the water's edge. Shuja, looking down, saw the head of the tiger emerging from behind a clump of bushes. Quietly, he nudged Zain and pointed downwards at the tiger.

Both of them brought the butt of their firearms to their shoulders. Gently Zain eased the cock of his matchlock back. The slight click immediately alerted the tiger, which retreated into the bushes, but a little while later, hunger and thirst overrode its caution. Again he emerged, but from a different direction, directly opposite Shuja and Zain. Shuja had also cocked his firearm and both of them waited.

Silently, placing each padded paw delicately forward, its body crouched, sniffing the air once or twice, the tiger moved towards the infant. When it was barely ten paces from the infant, and was gathering itself to pounce, Zain fired and the ball grazed the beast's right ear. At that instant, Shuja also fired and his shot hit the tiger squarely between the eyes. With a tremendous roar, the tiger rolled over onto its back, its paws vainly flailing in the air and then it lay perfectly still.

Tughril was the first to descend from the machan. Carefully he approached the tiger and checked if it was indeed dead. Then he looked up and said, 'Well shot, Sire. It is one of the largest tigers I have seen in my long years in shikar.'

'It was Nawabzada Saheb's shot,' said Shuja generously, thumping the beaming boy on the back. Both descended and stood around the animal as it was measured.

'Have the infant returned to its parents and give them this,' ordered Shuja as he peeled off two diamond rings from his fingers.

Meanwhile, some of the local villagers were hastily assembled, the tiger was trussed to a stout pole and a dozen men carried the dead animal, head swinging downwards, towards Shuja's camp. As Shuja approached his tent, the Captain of the Guard, Mahboob Alam, ran out and saluted.

'The Chief Wazir and some other nobles seek immediate audience, Sire,' he said, breathlessly.

'Now? Can't it wait till tomorrow?'

'They say it's most urgent, Sire.'

'Very well.'

'There are strong rumours circulating in the capital that His Imperial Majesty is no more,' announced Bismillah Khan in a sepulchral voice.

Five

'WHAT? ARE YOU absolutely sure?' Aurangzeb asked incredulously. At 39, Aurangzeb, third son of the Emperor and Viceroy of the Deccan, was of middle height, lean and wiry, with an oval face, and a thick black beard that hid a firm jawline. The mouth was thin-lipped and harsh, but the distinguishing features were his eyes, black as obsidian, which seemed to bore through like gimlets.

'There is absolutely no doubt of it, Highness,' replied Khuda Baksh, his intelligence agent in Shuja's court. He was a short, stout man with an open face.

The man had rushed from Dhaka to Aurangabad, Aurangzeb's capital, with a small escort of horsemen as fast as horses could carry them, and braving every conceivable obstacle, they had made the journey in a week. Immediately on reaching Aurangabad, Khuda Baksh had sought audience with Aurangzeb and now deep at night the two were huddled together.

'Prince Shuja has crowned himself as the Emperor, Your Highness. He has had the khutba read in his name in the mosques, and coins issued bearing his titles.' With weary fingers Khuda Baksh opened the inner flap of his travel-stained tunic, pulled out a handful of gold coins and placed them in his master's outstretched hand. Aurangzeb looked at them in the soft light of the candles. His agent was right. They were freshly minted, and bore the titles Shuja had taken.

'But was he not aware that the Emperor is recovering, and that he has been giving audience at the royal window for some time?'

'Either he was genuinely not aware of it, or he deliberately pretended not to be aware of it. The latter situation seems more probable. Of course rumours had been circulating in Bengal for the last few weeks that the Emperor was gravely ill. I am, however, informed that it was conveyed to Prince Shuja by some nobles at the close of a hunt, about twelve days ago, that His Majesty was rumoured to have succumbed to his illness. Prince Shuja returned to the capital immediately and proclaimed himself as the emperor. I thought the matter too important to be sent through normal channels and have carried the news myself.'

'You've acted correctly. You did well to undertake this arduous journey and report this matter, which is of the gravest importance, directly to us instead of relying on couriers. Of course our brother will no doubt be sending out his representatives to inform us of his...er...accession,' Aurangzeb could not keep the sarcasm out of his voice, 'but the information you have brought us so quickly, gives us invaluable time to formulate our own plans. You shall be well rewarded. Where does your zamindari lie?'

'In Rajshahi, Your Highness.'

'That's east of Rajmahal, isn't it?'

Khuda Baksh nodded.

'Well, that lies within the Bengal viceroyalty, and it is not within my power to make accretions to it, presently at any rate, and if you are gifted an estate in the Deccan, it may be difficult for you to manage, so you will have to make do with this.'

Aurangzeb wrote, signed and sealed an order to the Aurangabad treasury to pay Khuda Baksh 50,000 gold mohurs.

'Thank you, Your Highness. This is very generous of you,' said Khuda Baksh.

'Think nothing of it. Aurangzeb knows how to reward those who are faithful to him. Have you a place to stay here?'

'Yes, Your Highness. A close friend of mine is residing in Mehtab Bagh. I shall put up with him for the duration of my stay here. I shall also utilize this opportunity to get both ends of the courier service tightened.'

'Good. You know that you have access to us day or night. Whenever your courier comes with a message, bring him to us immediately, regardless of the time because it is necessary to keep abreast of all developments in Bengal, however insignificant they may appear to be.'

'Very well, Your Highness.' Khuda Baksh bowed and withdrew.

After Khuda Baksh had left, Aurangzeb began pacing the floor of his austere apartment. His brain was in turmoil. How could Shuja commit the incredible stupidity of declaring himself the emperor when Father was recovering, Aurangzeb thought. His secret agents had kept him posted regularly about every movement at the imperial court. He had been made aware of the progressive deterioration of the emperor's condition and then the improvement, reportedly through the ministrations of a vaid. Although Aurangzeb's antipathy towards Hindus was well known, he knew that some vaids possessed amazing skills in diagnosis and cure. There was little doubt that the emperor was recovering, and in these circumstances to declare oneself as the emperor was open rebellion. Shuja did not even have the law of primogeniture in his favour.

What could have induced Shuja to play his cards so early in the game, Aurangzeb wondered. He knew that Shuja did not lack intelligence, and was capable of vigorous action, but it was clear that his long residence in the moist, enervating climate of Bengal, coupled with his constant thirst for pleasure, had clouded his judgement and sapped his ability to think clearly. Not satisfied with Bengal, he now wanted the whole of Hindustan for his playground. Aurangzeb shuddered with distaste at the bizarre rumours he had been hearing about Shuja's ease-loving ways. *And such a man was now seeking dominion over the empire! By God! Come what may, we would not let even the shadow of such a man fall upon the throne.*

And what should be his own strategy now that Shuja had made the first move? The Emperor's illness was an indisputable fact and that he was now recovering also seemed very likely. What could have been the cause of the illness? Could it have been poison? Could someone in court, perhaps Dara himself, have tried to poison the Emperor? Extremely unlikely, thought Aurangzeb. After all what motive could Dara have had? Had not Dara always been the Emperor's favorite, and when recovery from the illness seemed dim, had not the Emperor communicated to the chief officers of the empire by signs that his heir was Dara? Furthermore, when recovery had begun, had he not heaped promotions and rewards on his eldest son? What about Jahanara or Roshanara then? Even less likely. Jahanara doted on her father, while Roshanara too loved her father in her own way. Any of the nobles then? That too was extremely unlikely, for Shah Jahan, though stern, was well liked and his age alone had by now cast him in the role of a father figure. No, the illness could only be ascribed to the hand of God and the subsequent recovery, probably, due to a vaid.

Now that Shuja had declared himself the Emperor, there was no doubt that a war of succession had started. Aurangzeb knew that it would be a fight to the finish. Delhi and Agra with their immense treasures were the prize, and if Shuja wanted to rule over all Hindustan, sooner or later he would have to march up the Gangetic valley to seize these two centres of Mughal power. Aurangzeb knew that supreme command of the imperial forces would rest with Dara, and reasoned that it would be his strategy to give battle to Shuja as far east as possible, to prevent him from linking up with the other two brothers. Aurangzeb had no high opinion of Shuja as a military commander, or of the troops under him, and was fairly certain that the imperial forces would crush them. But what, from his own point of view, was of paramount significance was that such a campaign would necessarily divert a considerable portion of the imperial military strength eastwards, and thus weaken the centre, perhaps so irretrievably that it would succumb to a determined assault.

To ensure doubly that the assault would be successful, it was necessary to make an alliance with Murad. Their combined armies would be able to sweep Delhi, but would Murad take the bait? Aurangzeb thought of his younger brother, six years his junior, with exasperation. Murad's impetuousness, lack of application, violent mood swings, sudden rages and above all his love of pleasure, hardly made him a dependable ally.

However, he was as brave as a lion. Aurangzeb knew that Murad too cherished visions of ruling the empire. He also knew that if for him an alliance with Murad was necessary, for Murad such an alliance was paramount. Indeed Murad would not be able to stir out of Gujarat, without coming to some accommodation with him, whose territories lay contiguous to Murad's own. *Yes*, thought Aurangzeb, *Murad would certainly be most eager for such an alliance, but let the initiative come from him. If I, Aurangzeb, move first in the matter, Murad will interpret it as a sign of weakness. Till then, the best course of action was to wait and watch.*

As dawn broke, Aurangzeb stopped pacing. He sat down on a divan and looked out of the open window at the grim battlements of Aurangabad fort, which were gradually coming into view. In another hour or so, the daily grind would commence—the state papers, the execution warrants, the muster rolls, the revenue records, the meetings and interviews with commanders and senior officials, and God knew what else. Would there ever be any end to this? *Pull yourself together*, Aurangzeb told himself. *He was born to be a king, and unremitting labour was the price of kingship.*

Like some others, Aurangzeb had cultivated the ability to sleep at will. He closed his eyes, stretched out on the bed and in an instant was fast asleep. Exactly half a watch later, he got up completely refreshed. Swiftly he performed his ablutions, bathed and after completing his prayers, was ready for the first caller of the day.

'My Lord, Mir Jumla prays to be received,' said the uniformed attendant.

'Just the person we wanted to see,' smiled Aurangzeb. 'Show him in.'

A Persian adventurer, Mir Jumla had begun life as a trader, and had migrated to Golconda, where his manipulative skills and capacity for intrigue had brought him to the notice of the ruler, Qutub Shah. In time, he became that sovereign's first minister, but not content with that, his vaulting ambition and administrative abilities had propelled him to carve out for himself a semi-independent principality in the Deccan. After Golconda fell to the Mughals, Mir Jumla had switched sides and pledged his loyalty to the Emperor. Upon being appointed a high minister by Shah Jahan, he had ben sent to the Deccan as Aurangzeb's principal adviser. However, Dara was aware of Mir Jumla's close proximity to his brother, and now that it was Dara who wielded authority, Mir Jumla's standing at court had weakened.

'Ah, welcome Mir Saheb,' said Aurangzeb as he went forward to receive him. 'You have come at an opportune moment. We were just thinking of you.'

'To what am I indebted for such an honour?' asked Mir Jumla smilingly, a tall, corpulent man, with a podgy face and restless, shifty eyes, but with a voice that was smooth and mellifluous, like oil gliding over silk.

'We have received unimpeachable intelligence that our brother Shuja has crowned himself as the emperor.'

'What? But the Emperor is very much alive. In this connection I wanted to give Your Highness some news of my own. On what basis has Prince Shuja crowned himself emperor when the emperor still lives, and when in any case he is not the eldest son?'

'It seems that he was told by his nobles about rumours that the Emperor had succumbed to his illness, and believing them to be true, or at any rate, wanting to believe them, he has assumed imperial trappings early last week. Doubtless his messengers must be on their way to spread the good word. In any case, not being the eldest son has never deterred any Mughal prince from making a bid for the throne.' Aurangzeb smiled thinly. 'What news have you brought?'

'My son, Mohammed Amin, who represents me in Delhi, has been barred from court. He has sent a coded message to me by fast courier, saying that Prince Dara has despatched a letter to you in the Emperor's name recalling me to Delhi, as soon as Perendha fort is captured. If I resist the recall, I am to be imprisoned by Your Highness and sent to Delhi in chains. The letter should be reaching here any hour now.'

'Arrest you? Has our brother taken leave of his senses?' Both men laughed. Then, Aurangzeb said, 'On a serious note, let the seige of Perendha be kept dragging. Later, if our brother still insists on your recall and arrest, we shall write to say that it has been complied with, and you are in our protective custody.'

After a thought, Aurangzeb said, 'As we see it, this claim of overlordship by our brother Shuja has deranged the entire political dynamics of Hindustan. Civil war is now inevitable, and sooner or later, Shuja will move his armies towards Delhi and Agra. Dara will endeavour to defeat Shuja quickly and as far in the east as possible, so that any threat to the capital is removed and imperial authority is reasserted.'

'Is Your Highness contemplating going to the aid of one or the other?' asked Mir Jumla, after a long pause.

Aurangzeb looked steadily into the Mir's eyes. 'No,' he said at length. 'We are too hard put to keeping order in these provinces and consolidating our earlier conquests, to think of venturing out. Our only pious hope and prayer is that the emperor is well and is allowed to perform his royal duties freely.

Of course to ensure that it is so, and he is not in our brother Dara's custody, we may pay a…er…visit to the Emperor, some time in the not-too-distant future, after our brothers Dara and Shuja sort out their problems amongst themselves.'

'When Your Highness pays this…er…visit, it may be helpful if Prince Murad were to accompany you. I am fairly certain that he also intends to pay a visit, and for him at any rate Your Highness' company would be of the first importance.'

'We are also thinking on the same lines, but we would like the initiative in this regard to come from him. It's however so difficult to get his mind focused on affairs of state.'

'Well, the prince's mind appears to get wonderfully focused, when it comes to murdering ministers,' replied Mir Jumla dryly. 'I gather that he ran a spear through old Ali Naqi just the other day. And presently his whole energies seem to be concentrated on a girl that was sent to him from Surankot. She's marvellously beautiful, I am told.'

'Not the Ali Naqi who was posted in Kandahar?' asked Aurangzeb. Inwardly, he was seething. He prided himself on his intelligence service and yet these important nuggets of news had to come from Mir Jumla, and not from his own agent in Murad's court, Arshad Rashid. Did Rashid require to be replaced? He promised himself to give the matter some thought.

'The same one. Honest to the core, but opinionated and arrogant. However, he didn't deserve the type of death he got,' replied Mir Jumla.

'No, he didn't. He had worked with us for some time and we found him a man of integrity. Such people are hard to find these days,' said Aurangzeb.

Mir Jumla paused for a while and then said, 'Your Highness, I see a way of getting Prince Murad to act quickly.'

'How?'

'His men keep moving between Delhi and Ahmedabad all the time. Let a letter, purportedly written by Prince Dara to Prince Shuja, fall into their hands in which Prince Dara proposes an alliance between himself and Prince Shuja against Prince Murad and you. I am sure that when Prince Murad sees such a letter, he will come rushing to you for an alliance.'

'But now that Prince Shuja has declared himself emperor, won't our brother Murad suspect that it is only a ruse?'

'The knowledge that Prince Shuja has declared himself emperor has still to percolate throughout the empire. This letter can be antedated a little before the event and a fast rider can carry it to Delhi, where the courier can arrange to be caught by Prince Murad's men. I do not think he will suspect anything, and after Ali Naqi's brutal death, his nobles are too afraid to speak.'

Aurangzeb fastened his gaze on Mir Jumla. 'No wonder they call you the "Fox of the Deccan",' he said. 'And what would you expect if you stand by our side in the ensuing war for the throne of Hindustan?'

'I have already pledged my allegiance to Your Highness. It is my earnest prayer to see Your Highness on the throne, and I shall claim my reward on that auspicious occasion,' replied Mir Jumla, smilingly as he rose. Aurangzeb rose along with him and accompanied him to the door. He caught the minister's shoulders with both his hands, and looked up into Mir Jumla's eyes. 'Inshallah! May that day come soon,' he said, his eyes glittering.

After Mir Jumla had left, Aurangzeb cancelled all appointments for the day and told his staff to keep the state papers away till he called for them. He needed time to decide how to put Mir Jumla's suggestion into operation. After a while, he sent for Allauddin Khan, his confidential agent who had come from Delhi the previous day with reports of the Emperor's medical condition and was to return back in a day or two. Allauddin, a slim, wiry, looking agent, was very fertile in resource.

'Khan Saheb, who is the best forger in Delhi?' Aurangzeb asked Allauddin, when he was shown in.

'There is a man called Inder Mohan Mathur, Your Highness. He runs a shop selling scrolls and parchments, and of course paper for land deeds and other documents. For a fee, he also records whatever the document is required to contain. His calligraphy is so perfect that people have difficulty in accepting that he is not among the Believers. In the process of mastering Farsi calligraphy, he has also perfected the art of forging signatures. Believe me, if he were to forge your signature, Your Highness, you would have difficulty in distinguishing which was the real signature, and which was the false one.'

'Excellent. That is just the type of man we need. Now, another point. Can you get access in Delhi to a blank sheet of the imperial stationery, which would normally be used by our brother Dara in his correspondence, and also his seal? The seal would be required only for a little while.'

Allauddin Khan thought for a few moments and then replied, 'That should not be too difficult, Your Highness. Lord Dara's record-keeper happens to be the relative of a close friend of mine, and it should be quite easy for him to do so. Of course, he will demand a consideration for it.'

'Give him whatever he asks for. Now here is what needs to be done. We shall dictate a letter purportedly written by our brother Dara to Lord Shuja, proposing an alliance against our brother Murad and ourselves. This letter will be transcribed by you on a piece of muslin and concealed in this little pouch here.' Aurangzeb handed a piece of muslin and a small pouch made of silk to Allauddin. 'You will proceed to Delhi tomorrow at first light, and on reaching there you will have the letter transcribed on the stationery used by Lord Dara in his correspondence. Get this Mathur to forge Dara's signature on the letter, and his seal should also be affixed thereon. Someone disguised as an imperial messenger must be made to look as if he's carrying this letter from Delhi to Bengal, and near Delhi itself, it should be allowed to fall into the hands of Prince Murad's men. If on the journey to Delhi, you yourself are intercepted, then before the pouch falls into the wrong hands, it should be destroyed.'

'Yes, Your Highness.'

'Good. Now as an added precaution, this letter shall be written by you here and carried in code. When you get to Delhi, you will transcribe it in Farsi. You are familiar with the Masnavi Code, are you not?'

Allauddin Khan nodded.

The code was simple and practically unbreakable, except by someone who was well versed in cryptology. It had been devised by Aurangzeb himself to communicate with his confidential agents, all of whom had received training in it.

'Now sit down here. Take this paper, quill and pot of ink. We shall dictate the letter in plain language, which you will take down on the paper and then transcribe it in code on the muslin given to you.'

After Aurangzeb saw that Qasim was comfortably seated he began dictating.

Our illustrious brother, dear as our own heart,

Greetings! We trust that by the grace of almighty Allah, this letter will find you in the best of health and spirits, and the people under your benign governance continue to flourish, for the greater glory of Islam and the prosperity of the empire.

As you are aware, our respected father had been suffering from indisposition for some weeks past, and our messengers have been keeping you abreast of his condition from time to time. Merciful providence has been kind to us, and we are happy to send you the pleasant news that His Majesty is now well on the way to recovery. The fever that had gripped him has disappeared, the pain and swelling in his limbs has largely subsided, the strength in his body is returning and he has been pleased to give audience at the royal window on a regular basis for some days now.

Yet amidst the joy that it gives us in communicating this good news, there is a tinge of sadness at the fact that hearing of our respected father's illness, our abandoned brothers have made known their evil designs to wrest the throne forcibly. This crime, and indeed it is nothing less than that, is all the more heinous when His Majesty's recovery is proceeding well and he is performing his royal duties.

Dear brother! Nothing is dearer to us than the continued long life of His Majesty, and the integrity and tranquility of the empire, which is a beacon of Islam and under whose benevolent canopy the children of Hindustan dwell in peace and harmony. By the same measure, nothing would grieve us more than to see this empire rent by civil war because of the warped ambitions and machinations of members of our own blood. Such attempts to disrupt the peace and tranquility of the empire must be crushed mercilessly and they can be defeated only if both of us present a solid united front and show to the world through an unshakeable alliance that no attempt to disturb the peace of the realm would be countenanced.

We await your response to this proposal and if you agree in principle, further details could be worked out.

Aurangzeb paused for a while. Should he refer to a future partition of the empire, between Dara and Shuja? He decided against it. Even a dim-witted person like Murad would realize that Dara would hardly suggest a partition when he considered himself the undisputed successor, and Murad's suspicions might well be aroused. The objective of the letter was only to get Murad to propose an alliance and what was already contained in the letter was sufficient.

Aurangzeb continued, 'End the letter by saying, "With renewed assurances of our consideration and heartfelt affection". The signature and seal of Lord Dara will have to be affixed at the bottom.'

'Yes, Your Highness,' replied Allauddin.

Aurangzeb ran hs eye over the draft. It was in order 'Fine. Now transcribe it in code in my presence on a piece of paper before you put it on muslin. Meanwhile I shall attend to my papers.'

As Allauddin worked laboriously, encoding the letter on the paper, Aurangzeb called for the official papers requiring disposal. After some time, noting that Allauddin was putting away Rumi's Masnavi, he asked, 'Have you finished the coding?'

'Yes, Your Highness,' replied Allauddin

'Let us see' he said. Taking the paper from Allauddin's hand, he opened the relevant page of the Masnavi and checked a few entries. He found them to be correct. The coding had been a laborious exercise and now it was well past noon. 'Well, things seem to be in place,' he remarked, as he returned the paper to Allauddin. 'Now copy this coded letter onto the muslin.'

It took another two watches for Allauddin to complete the task, after stretching the muslin tight, and writing the figures on it in a microscopic hand, with a pointed piece of lead. Meanwhile, Aurangzeb went through his papers with that ferocious concentration of which only he, among the Mughal princes, was capable of.

'The work is done, Your Highness,' said Allauddin stretching out from his cramped position at last and handing the muslin to Aurangzeb, who compared some of the entries in it with those on the paper and then handed the muslin back to Allauddin, after tearing the paper into little shreds. Allauddin inserted the muslin into the pouch, and then tucked it into the inner pocket of his tunic.

'Now, to repeat. You shall proceed to Delhi latest by first light tomorrow, and if all goes well, you should reach there within eighteen days. Get hold of that Mathur and have the letter decoded and transcribed on the imperial stationery with Lord Dara's signature and the imperial seal thereon. Have the letter fall into the hands of Lord Murad's messengers as soon as possible thereafter. Giving a leeway of say three to five days after you reach Delhi to procure the imperial stationery, and the seal, and to get the transcription done, it is expected that you would be able to get the letter fall into the hands of Lord Murad's men between the twenty-first and twenty-third day from today. As soon as they get hold of it, they will doubtless rush to Ahmedabad, which they should reach within eleven days or so. We would therefore expect some reaction from Lord Murad to reach us within thirty-six to thirty-eight days from today, reckoning the travel time from Ahmedabad to here by the swiftest means to be about four days. Knowing him, we are sure that his reaction will be instantaneous, and we will not have to wait beyond that period of time for it.'

'That is my own estimation, Your Highness'

'Now, do you have any doubts about what is required of you? If you have then speak up freely and clarify them, so that nothing is left vague and ambiguous. It need hardly be mentioned that if there is any real threat of the muslin falling into the wrong hands, it should be destroyed immediately.'

'I am quite clear about my task, Your Highness. I shall leave tomorrow morning at first light and ensure that everything is carried out as desired.'

'How are you for funds?'

'Enough to get me till Delhi. The office there will require replenishment.'

'That shall be done. You shall take a letter to Seth Bihari Mal here. He will issue a hundi to his cousin Seth Giriraj Mal, who operates a counting house in Chandni Chowk in Delhi. On receipt of the hundi, Seth Giriraj Mal will release the money to you. Will, say, a lakh mohurs be sufficient?'

'More than sufficient, Your Highness.'

Aurangzeb scribbled a few lines on a piece of paper asking the Aurangabad banker to issue a hundi in favour of his cousin in Delhi, and recoup the money from the local treasury. He signed it, and then taking a blob of melting red wax, sealed it with his signet ring before handing it to Allauddin.

'How many men will you take with you in your escort?' asked Aurangzeb.

'The same number, I brought with me, Your Highness—five.'

'Don't you think that the number is too few? After all, the distance is nearly four hundred kos, and the route is hazardous.'

'A large group will only delay me, Your Highness. Moreover, it will make us all too conspicuous. A caravan of merchants is departing for the north tomorrow and my companions and I shall travel with them for at least part of the way. As the merchants move in armed convoys, we shall be assured of protection for the period we are with them.'

'Whatever you think and decide is fine by me. We are only interested in ensuring that the objective is achieved.'

'That shall be ensured, Your Highness. There is one small matter. After Mathur commits the forgery, he may brag about it to others. What would Your Highness like done to prevent that?'

'Kill him,' replied Aurangzeb quietly.

Six

'THAT MENDACIOUS, DECEITFUL idolator,' spat out Murad, brandishing the letter in his hand.

He and Buland were closeted in Murad's private apartments. The forged letter had fallen into the hands of Murad's men near Delhi and they had rushed it to Ahmedabad. Reading the contents Murad exploded with anger, 'Seeks an alliance with Shuja to deny us our rightful inheritance, does he? He shall be taught a lesson that he will never forget. Merely because he is the emperor's favorite and also happens to be the eldest son does not automatically make him the heir. We Mughals, follow the maxim of "Takht-ya-Takhta". So it was in the days of our forefathers and so will it be now. In any case, our brother Dara is not man enough to hold the empire together. To think of it, Buland, neither are our other two brothers.'

'Ssshhh...Sire, I beg you not to express your feelings so openly. Remember, even walls have ears, and what is spoken here, even in jest, may well travel to the palaces of Delhi.'

'Do you think we care about what they think there?

You know Buland, Dara is slowly but steadily poisoning the Emperor. The person who is giving audience at the royal window is somebody made to look like the Emperor. That is why no durbar has been held since His Majesty took ill, and access to him is still very restricted. Don't think we are unaware of what is going on.'

'But what about your own confidential agent in Delhi, Sire, Mir Nasrullah Khan? Surely his report cannot be discounted.' By now Buland was beginning to feel that there may be some truth in the report.

'We have not heard greater rubbish in our life. Had you yourself not suggested that the Mir could have been purchased by our brother Dara? Can you ever imagine some Hindu entering the most private apartments of His Majesty and examining him, touching him? "Short stature", "piercing eyes" are all the figments of an overheated imagination. Utter drivel! We propose to settle accounts with the Mir, the next time we meet him. We shall be satisfied that His Majesty is alive and well, only after we personally set eyes on him. Till then, we shall proceed on the basis that he is either no more, or at any rate is permanently incapacitated. But coming back to this letter, how has this brother of ours—indeed, we are ashamed to call him our brother—the temerity to seek an alliance with Shuja against us and think that it would go unchallenged?'

'The letter might be a forgery, Sire. Would it not be better to get its authenticity secretly and independently verified through our sources in Delhi?'

'Forgery, Buland? Are you out of your mind? Sometimes we think that your impotence has affected your brain too. Who in God's name would want to, or for that matter, could forge such a letter? Can't you see that it bears the watermark of the imperial stationery office; it uses the ink which only the imperial records office is allowed to use, and it bears both Dara's signature as well as the imperial seal?'

'Sire, for all we know it may be Lord Shuja himself who has had this letter forged to give the rest of the world the impression that with this alliance he would be invincible. As Your Highness knows, there is talk in the city that Lord Shuja has crowned himself emperor, and such a proposal for an alliance purported to come from Lord Dara would lead others to conclude that the might of Delhi has been allied to the wealth of Bengal. There is also the chance that the letter has been forged at the instance of Lord Aurangzeb, to throw Your Highness into his embrace.'

'We cannot rely on this sort of bazaar gossip. We refuse to believe that our brother Shuja has crowned himself emperor. He's much too pleasure-loving for that sort of decisive action and the long years of residence in Bengal as Viceroy has further sapped his will. How can a man such as him think of rebelling against the Emperor? No, rebels require to be made of sterner stuff. So, put that out of your head. With regards to our brother Aurangzeb, yes, he has both the will and the daring to do so. But what would he gain by forging such a letter? Out of the four brothers, we two have been closest to each other, and now that our viceroyalties are adjoining, we consult each other regularly. Why should he forge this letter? If he wants an alliance with us, he could come out openly and ask for one, couldn't he?'

Buland looked at his master pityingly. He took in the bloodshot eyes, the flaring nostrils, the weak, irresolute mouth. *You fool,* he thought. *You poor benighted fool! While you are wallowing in drink and opium, and spending the waking hours between the legs of nubile virgins, your enemies are weakening the ground under your feet for the ensuing battle for the overlordship of Hindustan.* Buland was becoming fairly certain that the letter was a forged one and the forgery could have been committed at the instance of Aurangzeb. How he had managed it so far from his base, Buland was not sure, but it bore the stamp of Aurangzeb's craftiness.

They were interrupted by an attendant.

'An imperial messenger has come from Delhi, Sire. He bears an urgent message from the Emperor, and seeks immediate audience.'

Murad straightened up, and looked inquiringly at Buland. The eunuch shrugged his shoulders. 'Very well, show him in,' said Murad.

The messenger entered and bowed. His uniform was travel-stained and weariness showed on his face.

'Yes?' Murad asked.

The messenger silently pulled out a letter from the inner pocket of his tunic. Buland received the letter on a salver and carried it to Murad.

'Open and read it,' Murad told Buland, after asking the messenger to leave.

'It is not good news, Sire,' said Buland rapidly scanning its contents. 'The letter says that Lord Shuja has declared himself emperor, and his armies have crossed the frontiers of Bengal and are advancing upon Delhi. By doing this, he has put himself outside the pale of the ulema and will be treated as a rebel and crushed mercilessly. To deal with the developing situation, certain administrative changes have become necessary, one of which is that Your Highness has been transferred as Viceroy of Berar and some other nobleman is to be posted here.'

'The rascal!' whispered Murad, rising from his chair, red with rage. 'Clearly this is the work of our brother Dara. First he intrigues against us with our brother Shuja, and now he wants to set us at odds with our brother Aurangzeb. We see through his game clearly. If we obey, we shall surely come into conflict with our brother Aurangzeb, as Berar's boundaries which run contiguous with his own viceroyalty have not been clearly demarcated as yet, and moreover after Gujarat it is a mere molehill. On the other hand, if we do not obey, we will be treated as a rebel like our brother Shuja. What do you think we should do?'

'Sire, I am a humble eunuch and cannot dare presume to advise on such high matters of state. All I would suggest is that each move should be made only after its consequences are fully thought through.'

'Buland, you are only saying what is evident,' replied Murad testily. 'If you are not clear in your mind about what we should do, such doubts do not assail us. There is no question of our moving to Berar. Like our brother Shuja, we shall also march on Delhi, if possible in alliance with Aurangzeb, and if necessary, without him. By that time Dara and Shuja would have tired each other out. To justify our action, we shall give out that we believe the emperor is a helpless prisoner in Dara's custody, incapable of taking independent decisions and we have come only to set him free from the clutches of that unredeemed apostate.'

'My Lord, Aurangzeb will remain a thorn in Your Highness' flesh,' said Buland.

'We have thought about that too. Once Dara and Shuja are no longer serious contenders for the throne, we shall arrive at some arrangement with Aurangzeb. We think he should make a good Viceroy of Bengal. Till now he has served in the northwest and the Deccan. Let him get a taste of Bengal's mosquitoes. Moreover, the women there are reputed for their beauty, with long lustrous hair and soft skin. Unfortunately, his tastes do not run in that direction.' Murad's laughter echoed in the chamber. 'No, on a serious note, Bengal is the richest viceroyalty in the empire, and that should satisfy even his inordinate ambitions. Of course if he tries any mischief...' Murad lunged with a sword at an ornately carved wooden cupboard, piercing it before drawing it out again. 'You get our point, Buland?'

'Very well, Sire.'

'Now tomorrow, at noon arrange a meeting with Imam-ul-Mulk Imtiaz Beg, minister Pir Mohammed, Commander-in-Chief Qizl Baksh Khan, Master General of Ordnance Bughra Khan and Cavalry Commander Shahbaz Khan. They should bring with them up-to-date figures of the available forces, their disposition, the funds position and all other relevant materials. We would like their views on the action we propose to take.'

Next day, at the appointed hour, the officers filed into Murad's presence. Their subordinates waited in an antechamber with all the papers containing the details that might be asked for. Buland hung around in the background.

'You are aware of why we have sought your presence,' began Murad. 'As you know for some time past, His Majesty has been seriously unwell. Up to the last week or ten days, we were getting regular letters from our brother Dara about His Majesty's medical condition, but all of a sudden these letters have ceased. We can only fear the worst that either His Majesty is no more or is in our perfidious brother Dara's custody, and is unable to perform his royal duties. Meanwhile not content with imprisoning the Emperor—indeed we are fairly certain that Dara has been subjecting His Majesty to slow poison—he has proposed an alliance with our brother Shuja against us, and is also trying to set us at odds with our brother Aurangzeb. With this end in view he has had an order issued in the emperor's name transferring us to Berar, which we have no intention of obeying. Furthermore, we have received intelligence that our brother Shuja has declared himself Emperor and is marching towards Delhi. Unless we act promptly, we will lose the initiative.'

'What exactly does Your Highness have in mind?' asked Imtiaz Beg.

Buland had apprised them of the purpose of the meeting. Before coming, the senior officers had discussed the matter between themselves and had decided to dissuade Murad from embarking on so foolhardy a venture. Buland had told them of his own failure to dissuade Murad. His senior officers, all except Shahbaz Khan, still thought it their duty to make another attempt in this direction. They had chosen Imtiaz Beg as their spokesman, as he was the senior-most of those present, and Murad may heed to his wisdom.

'Why, hasn't Buland told you? We propose to march on Delhi, preferably in alliance with our brother Aurangzeb, but if absolutely necessary, even without him. We believe that the Emperor is no more, or at any rate so enfeebled and so completely in Dara's grip that he is incapable of taking decisions for the benefit of the empire. It is therefore our sacred duty to rescue him from Dara's control. As Dara and Shuja would have been weakened beyond measure, fighting amongst themselves, it should be a relatively easy matter to take Delhi.'

'Your Highness,' began Imtiaz. Knowing his master's

mercurial temper, he was not sure how Murad would react, but then taking the bit between the teeth, he plunged on. 'Buland has told us of the purpose of this meeting and my colleagues will place the resources' position in terms of men and material before you, as desired, but before coming here we had discussed the matter amongst ourselves, and felt it our duty to place certain facts for your kind consideration.'

'What are those?' asked Murad, with a slight sneer.

'His Majesty, the Emperor, still lives and according to reports, his health is improving by the day. Any attempt to march on Delhi will not only be open rebellion against the empire, but will violate the basic tenets of our faith, which enjoins on all believers to respect their parents and come to their aid in case of necessity. Here Your Highness, will be doing just the opposite.'

'What did our grandfather do against his father, Emperor Akbar? What did our own father do against his father, Emperor Jehangir? Where were those tenets of which you speak of, then? No Jenab Imtiaz, these arguments make no impression on us. Moreover it's a lie to say that the emperor's condition is improving. As we mentioned, the Emperor is either no more or is so severely incapacitated that he is unable to perform his royal functions and is a mere tool in Dara's hands. We are sure that Dara is doing his worst to ensure that the emperor departs from this world, so that he himself can ascend the throne. It will be a sad day for the empire when that happens. Indeed our religion, our culture, our very way of life will be thrown into jeopardy if that apostate, that idolator ever becomes emperor. Moreover, as we said, we shall tell the world that we are going north, only to satisfy ourselves that the emperor is alive and well and to rescue him from Dara's illegal confinement. Will we thereby not be going to his aid?' Murad laughed at his own cleverness.

'Very well, Your Highness. But let no one say that this old man of 79 years did not point out the folly of such a decision. I beg to retire.'

For a few seconds there was absolute silence in the room. All those present recalled what Murad had done to Ali Naqi, and their eyes lowered. They were apprehensive whether the same fate would befall Imtiaz. Murad's mouth tightened and it seemed that he was about to strike Imtiaz a blow, but with great difficulty he controlled himself. The spasm of rage passed.

'You may go,' said Murad coldly.

Imtiaz bowed and withdrew.

'Any other contrary views?' Murad asked sarcastically, his eyes sweeping over those present. None spoke or even dared to raise their heads. Eyes lowered, they stood silently. *Worms*, exulted Murad silently. *These were nothing but miserable little worms before him. Today he was Viceroy of Gujarat! Tomorrow he would be Emperor of Hindustan!*

'Good. Now what is the troop position?'

One by one the officers placed before Murad the strength of the troops under their respective commands, the resources' position and their additional requirements, particularly for weapons, which were duly noted.

'There is one suggestion I have for Your Highness' consideration,' said Pir Mohammed as the meeting was drawing to a close.

'Any suggestion would be welcome provided it is not defeatist,' said Murad.

'Your Highness, such a campaign will be an expensive proposition. Although the war material seems more or less adequate, our financial resources will not permit such an extended campaign so far from the borders of the viceroyalty, unless our funds are immediately augmented. I propose that the imperial mint and treasury in Surat be seized, and the merchants there be forced to extend a loan to finance the campaign.'

'An excellent idea,' said Murad, his eyes lighting up. 'We draw our salaries from there in any case. We can always justify our actions by saying that we had only gone to Surat to collect our salaries but the Qiladar of the fort there, upon Dara's instructions, shut the gates in our faces and opened fire upon us, compelling us to act in self-defence. Shahbaz, how soon can you proceed to Surat, with the siege train and other paraphenalia? Although strictly speaking, this is not the job of a cavalry commander, we are asking you because you have the reputation of being able to get things done.'

Shahbaz's chest swelled with pride. 'I can leave with the siege train within four days from today, Your Highness,' he replied. 'It will take another three weeks to reach Surat. Taking the fort will be difficult as it is surrounded on three sides by the sea, and the landward side bristles with cannon and swivel pieces. The treasury and the wealth of most of the rich merchants is stored for safe keeping in the fort. Even so, I am confident that I shall make the fort capitulate within two to three weeks of reaching Surat.'

'Good. Take as many troops and cannon as you want to lay siege to that city. Remember, we want every coin they have in Surat. Don't show any softness to those fat merchants, sitting on their gaddies there. They have fattened on the blood of the peasants, and deserve no sympathy. We shall set a target date for the launching of this northern expedition. Let it be three months hence, which will give enough time for all the preparations to be made foolproof. We shall review the preparations made in this regard myself from time to time. Meanwhile, we will open negotiations with Aurangzeb,but even if he does not join us, that should not deter us from this cause. Needless to say, these preparations and the deliberations of this meeting must be kept absolutely secret, till we ourselves give the word. Now, are there any questions or doubts?'

The officers looked at each other and then slowly shook their heads. One by one, they filed out of the room.

As the first camel-loads of the wealth from Surat began to reach Ahmedabad, with the promise of much more to come, Murad's elation knew no bounds. He knew that his difficult financial position would ease substantially, and it was time to do what he had wanted all this while.

Summoning Pir Mohammed, he said, 'The progress of brother Shuja continues unabated, and having proclaimed himself Emperor of Hindustan, scores of local chieftains are said to be flocking to his standard. Lest he seizes the initiative from us, and our just claims go by default, we should not lose more time in marching towards Delhi. We had set a target date for the northern expedition three months since we had conferred last, but Shuja's progress requires us to draw the date closer. Let the court astrologers be brought before us to advice on an auspicious date and time for us to embark on this momentous enterprise.'

Next day, the three senior court astrologers were brought trembling into Murad's presence. 'You know why you have been sent for,' Murad began without preamble. 'It is our unalterable will to set free our emperor from the clutches of an apostate, so that the empire is finally rid of the enemies of our faith and power no longer reposes in the hands of idolators. Consult amongst yourselves, and advise us on the most auspicious date and time for embarking on this enterprise. Make sure that your advice is unanimous. We want no time wasted in futile dissensions and wrangling. We have heard that no two soothsayers can agree amongst themselves. Well, we have a sure remedy for that, which you will disregard at your peril.' Drawing his sword from its scabbard, he slashed at a golden flagon of wine that stood close by, sending it skeetering across the parqueted floor, its contents spilling all over the place.

The three petrified old men wanted to put a thousand kos between themselves and their capricious master. Finally Mian Ali Zaqi, the senior-most of them, found the courage to speak. In a quavering voice, he said, 'Your Highness, Pir Saheb had told us the purpose of our being summoned before your august presence and we had the opportunity of holding consultations amongst ourselves. As in Your Highness' case Mars is the lord of the ascendant, our almanacs tell us that the most auspicious hour for embarking on this momentous enterprise will be half a watch after sunrise in exactly eleven days from now. Such a conjunction of favourable planets will not be seen again for a very long time.'

Murad looked from one to the other. 'Are all agreed on this?' he asked, as if daring the others to take a different view. All nodded humbly, eyes lowered.

'So be it then,' Murad said.

Then Pir Mohammed spoke in his most persuasive style, 'Your Highness, eleven days gives us hardly enough time to organize the expedition on the scale that will be required to ensure its success. If Your Highness approves, let the function eleven days from now be a restricted one, so that we do not lose the favor of the stars, and Your Highness' intention will not be in doubt. The public announcement of that intention may be made after all the necessary arrangements are made, by which time all the wealth of Surat would also have reached us.'

Murad saw that this advice was eminently practical, and he agreed. At the auspicious hour and day, in the presence of a few selected officers to whom extravagant promises of yet higher posts and rewards were made, he proclaimed his intention of leading an expedition to Delhi. As the machinery to organize the expedition moved into high gear, all that now remained was to fix the date for its departure.

Seven

'THE IDIOT,' FUMED Aurangzeb, as he held Murad's letter announcing his intention to lead an expedition to Delhi for what he termed 'rescue of the Emperor'. 'Despite all our advice to him not to do anything that might arouse suspicion, and instead to dissemble, to temporize, to write soothing letters to Dara protesting loyalty to the throne in the face of the open rebellion by Shuja, he has gone and done it'. Aurangzeb's eye quickly skimmed through the key phrases in the letter '...our beloved father is a captive of Dara...his actions in proposing an alliance with our brother Shuja to deny us our rightful share...Shuja is moving towards Delhi and we may already be too late...I am ready to advance...we can coordinate our plans...however before that, we should settle the terms of our partnership...'

Aurangzeb threw the letter away, and ran his hands over his face. Till now his plan had worked splendidly. Soon after Dara's forged letter had fallen into Murad's hands, he had received the first letter from his younger brother criticizing the perfidy displayed by Dara. Aurangzeb had replied to that letter guardedly, but in a manner that encouraged Murad to think that his elder brother shared his own opinion of Dara. Soon that exchange had led to a brisk correspondence between the two brothers, carried by special couriers stationed twelve miles apart.

While they had arrived at a broad understanding that they would act in concert, and do nothing without consulting each other. Aurangzeb had been continuously counselling Murad to exercise caution, lest the wrath of the imperial armies came down upon them. He had strongly advised against making any overt move till it was confirmed that the Emperor was no more. However, to the impetuous Murad such inaction was galling, and now he had taken the bit between the teeth.

Aurangzeb clapped his hands. An attendant appeared and bowed.

'We wish to confer with Mir Jumla and Nawab Iqbal Mohammed Khan, immediately. Also ask secretary Qabil Khan to be present,' Aurangzeb told the attendant. These were the officers closest to him, whom he had elavated for their ability and unswerving loyalty to him, and whom he often used as a sounding board whenever he wanted to clarify his own ideas.

When the noblemen had been shown in, Aurangzeb began, 'Are you aware that our brother Murad has decided to lead an expedition on Delhi?'

'When did this take place, Your Highness? In fact, with Lord Shuja having declared himself as the emperor, I was expecting this to happen sooner or later. But perhaps not quite so quickly,' Mir Jumla said.

'Four days ago. A courier has just brought a letter from Ahmedabad. It seems that the function declaring his intention was a restricted one and the public announcement will be held some time later, but he has made his intentions clear. All along, we had been counselling him not to take any hasty action, but to no avail. Without even confirming that the Emperor is no more, he has taken this step. What do you think we should do? Of course, officially we are free of suspicion as we have not done anything which might be construed as acting against the throne, but our closeness to our brother Murad is common knowledge. We know that many senior commanders are being recalled to Delhi from our viceroyalty, and officers handpicked by our brother Dara are being posted to Malwa and Gujarat. Dara knows that ultimately it is we who stand in the way of his imperial ambitions and not Murad or Shuja, and these moves are obviously designed to weaken us and to prevent us from effecting any kind of junction with our brother.'

There was silence in the room as each of the officers were immersed in their own thoughts. Then Mir Jumla sought permission to speak; Aurangzeb nodded.

'Your Highness, moments come in the lives of some rare individuals, which if seized by them can help change history. Such a moment is with us now. Even if the Emperor is recovering, there is no doubt that he is old and his days are numbered. After his departure, the empire will be in sore need of a strong hand which only Your Highness can provide. I say this not to flatter, but speak only the simple truth. As I see it, presently the imperial forces are already distracted by the invasion from the east, and now they face a threat from the southwest. In case the imperial forces defeat Lord Shuja in the east and return in time, it will be easy for them to turn on Lord Murad and Your Highness, whether you are acting jointly or separately. Similarly, if Lord Shuja is victorious and seizes Delhi, he will gather his strength and attack Lord Murad and

Your Highness, whether you both are in combination or acting singly. Whoever rules in Delhi will strive to their utmost to isolate Your Highness, because they realize that it is you who poses the greatest threat to their imperial ambitions. That trick of the letter from Lord Dara to Lord Shuja having worked, and Lord Murad having come to us for an alliance, we should seize this opportunity for fleshing out the understanding with him and prepare to launch a northern expedition with him well before either Prince Dara or Prince Shuja recover fully from their internecine war.'

'In the meantime, should not we also declare ourselves emperor?' asked Aurangzeb, with a wry smile.

'Heaven forbid, Your Highness,' said Mir Jumla, rolling his eyes in mock horror. 'At this rate, Hindustan may run out of crowns! There will be time enough for that, when Delhi and Agra fall to Your Highness.'

Aurangzeb looked at the other two. They nodded assent. Then Nawab Iqbal Mohammed Khan sought leave to speak. He was a thin, languid-looking man, with a razor-sharp intellect. 'I would like to supplement what Mir Saheb has said by adding that before we can embark on a northern expedition, we should arrive at some settlement with Bijapur and with Golconda.'

'We have been altogether too soft with these Bijapuris,' said Aurangzeb acerbically. 'After their defeat, we could have squeezed them dry, but the emperor himself remitted a third of the one-and-a-half crore mohurs indemnity that they were required to pay, and while the whole state from coast to coast would have been ours, they know that with the emperor in his present condition, the terms of the treaty will not be rigorously pressed. Even Perendha fort has not yet been ceded, and they are raising their heads again.'

'True, Your Highness, but when the rich plains of Hindustan beckon us, let us not concern ourselves unduly over a molehill. The settlement with Bijapur I propose is only a tactical ploy, so that our flank does not remain endangered when we proceed towards north.'

'What about Golconda?'

'Your Highness is aware that despite having been defeated, Qutb Shah is reluctant to give up the territory, which he is required to cede by the terms of the peace treaty. He has been dragging his feet in this regard. Although admittedly it is distasteful, I would humbly suggest that the matter be left as it is, till affairs work themselves out in the north. That may not be quite to the liking of my friend Mir Saheb here, whose interests in the Deccan are well known, and who is keen that we gain possession, but pressing Qutb Shah too hard to fulfil his treaty obligations may not be the most advisable course at this juncture, when it is vital to keep him quiescent. Once the north is secured, we can always tidy up these little pockets,' replied the Nawab.

Aurnagzeb looked quizzically at Mir Jumla.

The Mir, his jaw tightening, murmured, 'Nawab Saheb is right in pointing out that it is very necessary to keep our southern borders secure when we move north. For the rest, I leave the matter entirely in Your Highness' hands.'

'There is another chieftain, Your Highness whom it would be advisable to conciliate before a northern expedition is set in motion. I refer to Shiva Bhonsle, who is better known as Shivaji among his people,' said the Nawab smoothly.

'Yes, he's a young man who is as daring as he is resourceful. We propose to send a conciliatory reply to him in response to his message, but mark our words, he's one who will bear watching. Well, you have given us valuable advice, and we will think over your suggestions carefully.'

Aurnagzeb's counsellors bowed and withdrew. Never given to acting in haste, Aurangzeb mulled over the advice they had given him. At length he was forced to conclude that it made good sense—conditions were propituous for an advance on Hindustan, in conjunction with Murad, while Dara was facing an attack from the east. Even Murad's precipitate announcement of marching on Delhi could be turned to advantage by proclaiming that he, like any dutiful son, was proceeding to Delhi only to pay his respects to the Emperor who was recovering from a serious illness, and his presence along with Murad would only help restrain his impetuous younger brother. As for the army that would be behind him, well, they were there only to ensure that he was not blocked by those who did not want the son to meet the father.

In reply to Murad's request for a settlement of the terms of the partnership, Aurangzeb wrote smoothly '...my love and favour towards you will daily increase...and after the God-forsaken idolator has been overthrown...I shall keep our promise and after mutual consultation we shall arrive at a fair, just and equitable settlement as to the division of the provinces within the empire...'

Aurangzeb also wrote conciliatory letters to both Adil Shah of Bijapur and Qutb Shah of Golconda.

Meanwhile preparations for the northern expedition were mounted on a war footing by Aurangzeb and nothing was left to chance. The ferries across the River Narbada which marked the traditional border between Hindustan and the Deccan were seized, to prevent any news leaking out. Recruitment was stepped up. Lead, sulphur and saltpetre were purchased for making munitions. The possibility of encouraging the Persians to create a diversion in the west was explored, and correspondence was even initiated with Shuja away in the east for a possible coordination of plans.

Despite all the precautions taken, news of the preparations being made were like the rumblings of distant thunder, barely audible at first, but gradually gaining in intensity, and fed by rumours, they were beginning to be received in the imperial capital with increasing foreboding. Late one evening in early winter, Prince Dara sat grimly, holding several reports and letters he had received over the past few days. The Emperor sat before him, looking at the River Jumna from his apartment in Agra Fort to which he had moved from Delhi for a change of air. 'The contumacy of our brothers Murad and Aurangzeb is exceeded only by that of our brother Shuja,' said Dara. 'Despite Your Majesty informing them that you have now overcome your illness, and there is no need for them to leave their viceroyalties to come and see you, they have been writing letter after letter to say that they will not rest till they pay their respects to you in person. Pay their respects, indeed! They are planning nothing less than a full-scale invasion of Hindustan, and that too while we have not yet settled accounts with Shuja.'

'Why don't these sons of ours adhere to the principles of obedience and duty?' lamented Shah Jahan querulously. 'Have we not given them so much already? How could we have spawned such ungrateful sons? They are doing all this despite knowing that we have chosen you, being our firstborn, to succeed us. At least Aurangzeb has been more respectful.'

Dara gave a short laugh. 'Aurangzeb? He's the one from whom we have the most to fear. His letters drip with concern about Your Majesty's welfare, but doubtless it is he who is guiding Murad and is possibly intriguing with Shuja too.'

'What do you propose to do now?'

'Sulaiman with his army is already approaching Benares and if Shuja does not withdraw, we expect a battle there in the next few weeks. The troops are drawn from the best we have and we have sent two of our finest generals with Sulaiman. They will be enough to handle Shuja.'

'What about the south?'

'We propose to send Mirza Kasim Khan with an army to Gujarat to remove Murad forcibly, and another to Malwa under Raja Jaswant Singh of Marwar to replace Shaista Khan, whose loyalty is doubtful. The two armies will act in concert under the overall direction of Raja Jaswant Singh, to prevent Murad and Aurangzeb from combining forces.'

'Raja Jaswant? We have no doubts about his valour in battle and his qualities of leadership are well known but won't it be more...er...appropriate to give the overall command to Mirza Saheb?'

Dara realized at once what the Emperor was getting at. 'Sire, what would be a greater affirmation of the fact that the empire looks at both the Hindu and the Muslim with an equal eye, than the leadership of the army that might be called upon to measure swords against Your Majesty's own sons being placed in the hands of a Rajput? It will be one more strong link that will bind that warrior race to the cause of the empire.'

Shah Jahan was silent for a while. He shivered slightly, and pulled his shawl a little tighter around himself to keep out the chill . 'Well, we suppose so,' he said at length. 'However, there is one thing we want you to promise us.'

'Whatever you say, Sire. Every wish of yours is our command,' replied Dara.

'Dara, there shall be no shedding of your brothers' blood. Shuja, Murad and even Aurangzeb are terribly misguided, but in all of us runs the same blood, and we will not countenance the blood of one brother being spilt by another. All of you are the offspring of our dearly beloved Mumtaz. Oh, if she were here now, what good advice she would have given her sons! Who will profit from such a war between brothers? None, but our enemies. One spark is enough to set the whole of Hindustan in flames. Tell Sulaiman, Jaswant Singh and the other commanders that it is my command that their operations shall be entirely defensive. Once your brothers are seen withdrawing, they will disengage. Is that clear?'

'But that will tie down the hands of our commanders,' Dara expostulated. 'Murad, and perhaps even Shuja, might be persuaded to return to their viceroyalties, but not Aurangzeb. We hate to say this, but perhaps even you are not safe at his hands. Shirazi the Persian Ambassador sought audience with us the other day and hinted that Aurangzeb had even got Murad to write to the Shah of Persia to do some sabre-rattling on our western frontiers as a diversion. He will not even hesitate to get foreigners to interfere in our domestic quarrels, if he perceives that some personal advantage is to be had.'

'God forbid! You mustn't say such things about him, Dara. The Persian Ambassador must have misunderstood.'

'We speak the truth, Sire. Aurangzeb is insatiably ambitious and thinking that the time is ripe, he is readying himself to strike, from behind Murad's skirts. Mark our words, when it will suit him, he will discard Murad for his sole ambition is to rule over Hindustan, even if it means clambering over our dead bodies. We beseech you, Sire, let us give our commanders a free hand to deal with the situation as they think best.'

'Free hand, yes, but not when it comes to spilling the blood of your brothers. That must not happen. Shuja must be told to return to Bengal, and Murad and Aurangzeb must be told not to leave their viceroyalties. If they disobey, they may even be forcibly dispersed, but the moment they show signs of retiring, our forces should disengage. Promise us that, Dara.' Shah Jahan caught his son by both shoulders, and looked deep into Dara's eyes, as if he would wring the promise out of his son.

For a long while Dara was silent. He knew that the coming war of succession would be a fight to the finish. Yet here was his father imploring him to ensure that there would be no shedding of the royal blood. At length filial love and respect overbore his natural inclinations. 'Very well, Sire. We shall instruct our commanders accordingly, but we still feel we are making a grave mistake.'

Shah Jahan beamed. 'No, Dara. All will be well. We know our sons, and do you think we have ruled this empire for thirty years without being able to read men and matters like an open book? We are sure that once Murad and Aurangzeb see the imperial standards, they will retire and hopefully, Shuja too will fall back. After the situation normalizes, we shall work out a solution which will leave none dissatisfied.'

As Dara walked away from his father's apartments, he had the premonition that the promise would prove to be a disastrous folly, and its consequences would haunt him to the end of his days.

The removal of Shaista Khan as Governor of Malwa, who was an important communication link between Aurangzeb and Murad; the imperial summons recalling Mir Jumla to the capital; Murad's increasingly importunate letters, imploring Aurangzeb to act before it was too late; and the growing restiveness among his own adherents to act, on pain of forfeiting their loyalty if he delayed any further, convinced Aurangzeb that the time for laying his cards on the table was fast approaching.

As the whole of Hindustan slipped into deep winter, Aurangzeb scanned the horizon each day eagerly for authentic news of events in the imperial capital. If on one day a secret message arrived from a disaffected noble informing him that the Emperor's condition had sharply deteriorated and pledging allegiance to the viceroy of the Deccan as the future emperor of Hindustan, a day or two later, another letter of an earlier date would be received from one of his spies or agents in the capital, saying that the Emperor had fully recovered and was now attending to all his normal duties. What was he to make of all this welter of contradictory information?

Aurangzeb decided to wait and watch the events till his opponents made the first move. He had not long to wait. Word was brought by relays of fast couriers that Raja Jaswant Singh and Mirza Kasim Khan had left Agra with their armies within days of each other, and they were heading towards Ujjain to sit astride the northern road and thus bar any advance by Murad or Aurangzeb into Hindustan. The die was cast.

Eight

IT WAS THAT brief period when the chill winter winds that sweep the northern plains have abated, when the flowering trees and plants are in full bloom, when the earth wears a green mantle and when the scorching rays of the summer sun, which bake and blast the land, are still some months away, Aurangzeb set out with his 30,000 veterans from Aurangabad. He had sent the van of his army ahead to Burhanpur with his eldest son Mohammed Sultan a few days earlier, and as the great army wended its way northward, Aurangzeb was atlast at peace with himself. All the doubts and, anxieties had been sloughed off, and he was ready to face the outcome of his decision. To be sure he had not struck the imperial posture as yet, and to all intents and purposes he was just a dutiful son going to pay his respects to his father, but none could be fooled. The world knew that Aurangzeb had also thrown his hat into the ring and the Mughal empire would go to the one with the stoutest arm, and the sharpest sword. *Indeed, what other option did I have,* Aurangzeb asked himself. *To remain cooped up in the Deccan while the empire was up for grabs was to invite certain destruction, sooner or later. Better to wager one's all in a single throw of the dice, and perhaps gain the throne of Hindustan than die in some godforsaken corner of the Deccan.*

On reaching Burhanpur, a fortnight's halt was called and the military dispositions for the further advance finalized. It was in Burhanpur, late one night, as Aurangzeb lay in his tent that he heard some commotion. Parting the curtain flap, he came out, sword in hand.

'What is the matter?' he asked one of the guards, standing outside beneath a flaming torch.

'A messenger, Your Highness. He comes from the east and seeks audience.'

'Bring him before us at once.'

'Yes, Your Highness.'

A few minutes later, a messenger, almost half dead with fatigue, was led staggering into Aurangzeb's tent. His clothes were rent and his body displayed several bleeding injuries. He had been sent by Mubarak Beg, one of Aurangzeb's confidential agents in Shuja's court.

'Let him rest a little,' said Aurangzeb, as he saw the man settled in a chair and then with his own hand, gave him a goblet of wine to drink. When the man had regained his breath, still gasping, he reported, '...coming from Benares, Your Highness. My...Shuja has...beaten by...Sulaiman Shukoh...armies... flight.'

'Good God, man. Collect your wits about you, and then tell me all that happened in a coherent manner. Take some more rest if you want, and then recount everything from the very beginning.'

The man nodded humbly. After some time, when he had gained his composure, he spoke, 'I am coming from Benares,

Your Highness. I have ridden almost without stopping and have changed six horses on the way. My Lord Shuja has been decisively beaten by the imperial forces under My Lord Sulaiman Shukoh and his armies have been put to flight. So severe has been the defeat that Shuja barely escaped with his life, and on my way here, I heard that Sulaiman had chased him east of Patna.'

'Did Mubarak Beg not give you any written message?'

'No, Your Highness. He was some distance behind Shuja's forces, but the confusion was so great that he had no time to pen any written message. Moreover, he was apprehensive that if I was caught crossing the imperial lines, the message might prove incriminating. He only told me to report to you orally all that I had seen and heard, and trusted that my report would be faithful and accurate.'

'All right, what all did you see and hear?'

'Shuja's army had entrenched itself on the north bank of the Ganga about two kos northeast of Benares. For about two weeks there was desultory skirmishing. Meanwhile, Sulaiman had reconnoitered Shuja's military dispositions and noticed that discipline was lax, patrolling non-existent and even the frontline troops were lolling about. Early in the morning, nine days ago, under the pretence that the troops were being redeployed, the imperial forces fell upon Shuja's army. Some of his followers managed to seat him on his elephant and lead him away but most of his generals fled and only small groups of soldiers offered resistance. Shuja's army or what was left of it was being chased by Sulaiman eastwards.'

Aurangzeb's eyes gleamed. This suited his plans perfectly. With a sizeable chunk of the imperial forces together with several able generals tied up in the east, Dara's capacity to defend the empire's heartland would be that much weaker.

That night Aurangzeb tossed restlessly in his bed. Time, he realized, was of the essence and the odds would swing much more in his favour if he reached the Delhi–Agra axis where the decisive battle would be fought, before Sulaiman returned with his troops. Not a moment, therefore, was to be lost.

Early next morning, Aurangzeb summoned his senior commanders.

'Prince Shuja has been defeated by the imperial forces near Benares and is retreating eastwards,' began Aurangzeb. 'He is being pursued by Prince Sulaiman and it will take that young man at least eight weeks to return with his generals, troops and artillery to Agra. It is therefore imperative that we reach Agra before he returns, and in case Prince Dara challenges our presence, atleast he will not be able to draw comfort from Prince Sulaiman's forces. How soon can we get our men on the move?' he asked, turning to Khan-i-Zaman, the Inspector General of Ordnance.

'At least ten days, Your Highness,' answered the short, stocky officer who seemed to radiate energy. 'The wheels of most of the gun carriages have been torn off their axles, and require refitting after the journey from Aurangabad. We are woefully short of cannon balls, which are being cast in the foundries here, and as the elephants to draw the guns forward are also in short supply we are requisitioning oxen but the breed here is so small that they are practically useless when it comes to dragging the guns over long distances.'

Aurangzeb put the same question to the other generals, all of whom asked for about the same time to get their squadrons on the road.

'We march at dawn on the fifth day from today.'

'But, Your Highness.....' Khan-i-Zaman tried to interject.

'No, Khan Saheb,' murmured Aurangzeb courteously but firmly. 'We have full faith in you to get the artillery up and going within the time specified. And that goes for all of you.' He looked searchingly from one commander to the other. Under his penetrating gaze, they all dropped their eyes.

'Remember, the sooner we reach Agra, the greater our chance of success to deprive the imperial forces of reinforcements, in case they do try to bar our path.'

Five days later, the great army was on its feet again and was slowly wending its way northwards. Aurangzeb had left his father-in-law Shah Nawaz Khan to follow after three days to bring up the rear, but when he reached Mandwa, he received disquieting news.

'A courier has just come from Burhanpur, Your Highness,' said Nawab Iqbal Mohammed Khan after he had sought Aurangzeb's audience. 'He brings news that Lord Shah Nawaz Khan is deliberately lingering in Burhanpur, and has declined to march forward. He describes our expedition as open rebellion to which he will not be a party.'

'What?' cried Aurangzeb, in consternation. 'I cannot believe this. All along he wanted us to liberate our revered father from the clutches of that apostate. What could have led to this complete change of mind?'

'Doubtless, it's your advancing towards Agra, Your Highness,' said the courtier, wryly. 'It is a classic case of courage draining away as the moment of truth approaches.'

'What then should be done? Such behaviour may drive others also to abandon the expedition. At the same time, we cannot forget that he is our father-in-law, and is one of the leading noblemen of the empire.'

'I suggest comfortable internment of Khan Saheb in Burhanpur itself, Your Highness,' said the Nawab. 'He may be confined to his palace for the duration of the expedition. He may continue to enjoy all the privileges that he is used to, only his movements may be restricted and of course his meetings with outsiders.'

'And how would you suggest that this…er…internment be effected?'

'I suggest that Prince Mohammed Sultan be entrusted with this rather delicate task. He is well liked by Khan Saheb. The Prince needs to tell him that for a short while he will be confined to the palace, as reliable information has been received of threats to his life from assassins hired by Dara, who has got wind of his support for your expedition. No doubt, he will fulminate and may want to send you a message for his immediate release, which Prince Mohammed can gracefully agree to forward, but in case it does not get through it can always be said that the couriers were waylaid as they passed through the dense jungle. By the time one is allowed to get through, Inshallah our expedition would have been successful and Khan Saheb can be released with high honours and a generous increase in his estates, with a few apologies if necessary.'

Aurangzeb mulled over the advice. Yes, it seemed the best way to tackle the situation, he thought.

After the Nawab had left, Auranzeb sent for his son Mohammed Sultan. He reminded Aurangzeb of himself when he was twenty years younger.

'Shah Nawaz Khan Saheb has declined to join our expedition to Agra,' began Aurangzeb. 'He thinks we are revolting against our revered father. We must confess that we find this behaviour most strange, as it was he, more than anyone else, who was egging us on to free our father from the clutches of that apostate.' Aurangzeb was watching his son closely, trying to fathom to what extent his sympathies lay with Shah Nawaz Khan. Mohammed Sultan betrayed no emotion as he listened to his father.

'Proceed at once to Burhanpur,' Aurangzeb continued. 'On reaching there you will try to persuade him to join in the expedition, and bring him back with you, failing which he should be taken into protective custody, to avoid our plans being revealed. He should be detained in his palace within which he may enjoy all his accustomed privileges, but he will not be allowed to leave it and will not be permitted to communicate with any outsider. His messages, in case he chooses to send any, should be sent directly to us. A set of instructions is to be handed over to Muazzam Khan, the commander of the Burhanpur garrison, regarding the disposition of forces around the palace, should your persuasion fail. Hand them over to Muazzam and satisfy yourself that they are properly implemented. Leave while there is still light today. Take a strong escort party with you.'

'Very well, Sire.' Saying so, Prince Mohammed bowed and left the room.

After a short while, Aurangzeb clapped his hands and a flunkey appeared. 'Ask Imran Baksh to come here at once.' Within a short while, a slim man with alert eyes was ushered in. He was an agent in Aurangzeb's confidential section.

'We have sent Prince Mohammed on a mission to persuade our father-in-law to join us in our expedition to liberate our revered father from the foul clutches of our apostate brother Prince Dara, and if persuasion fails, to take him into protective custody lest news of our plans are leaked out. See that our instructions are carried out faithfully, and keep an eye on Prince Mohammed Sultan, lest he thinks it more worth his while to collude with our father-in-law. Take the fastest horses with you and reach Burhanpur before he does. Report to me personally all that you see and hear. Godspeed.'

Imran bowed and withdrew.

Jaswant Singh, in his march from Agra, had got wind of Murad's thrust from Gujarat ino Malwa and was receiving regular reports of Murad's advance. On reaching Ujjain by forced marches, he ordered a halt. He knew that if Murad's movement towards the north was to be checked, it had to be somewhere in that region.

On the third evening, after reaching Ujjain, his chief of staff Askaran Khan was shown into his pavilion. 'What tidings do you bring, Askaran?' Jaswant asked.

'Two additional squadrons of cavalry have joined Prince Murad's forces, My Lord, which brings his total troop strength to around ten thousand.'

Jaswant let out a hearty laugh. 'Ten thousand! Well that's far less than our own strength. The sight of our numbers will be enough to send him scurrying back and regretting that he ever had the temerity to raise his standard against the Emperor.'

'Even so, I don't like it, Your Excellency,' said the general. 'While we have been concentrating on Prince Murad's movements, we have no news of what Prince Aurangzeb is up to. It may be easy to deal with Prince Murad singly, but if Aurangzeb has also timed his advance to coincide with that of Murad, and the two effect a junction, it may be very difficult to stop them. Indeed, for all Prince Murad's rashness he would not be so foolhardy as to take on the might of the entire empire alone, leaving his entire eastern flank exposed, unless he has received some assurances of support from Aurangzeb.'

'Prince Aurangzeb?' Jaswant asked, dismissively. 'He is probably stitching skull caps in Aurangabad at this moment. Surely if he was marching northward, we would have got news of it. Are our spies not everywhere and are not the ferries across the Narbada well guarded?'

'True, Excellency, but somehow I feel that the two brothers are acting in concert and sooner than later, we are going to face formidable opposition.'

'You are unnecessarily apprehensive, Askaran. Even if Aurangzeb plans to march northward, he will still be hundreds of kos away and for the present we have only this hot-headed stripling before us, and the mere sight of our forces will make him retire.'

Just then an orderly entered Jaswant Singh's pavilion. 'There is a Brahnin pandit who seeks immediate audience with you, Excellency,' he said.

'Brahmin pandit?' exclaimed Jaswant, as Askaran Khan bowed himself out. 'Here? What can he want at this hour? Show him in.'

The orderly turned around and went out for a brief moment only to return with a tall, striking man clad in a white dhoti with three horizontal caste marks on his forehead.

'Welcome, Maharaj,' said Jaswant, bowing low and offering the Brahmin a seat on the masnad. 'To what do we owe the honour of this visit? You had only to command me and we would have presented myself before you without you taking the trouble to come all this way. Incidentally, Maharaj, where is your hermitage? My men did not tell me about the presence of one as exalted as you anywhere in the vicinity.'

'From where I come is only of slight importance, but the message I carry is of the gravest import. Why do you get into the quarrels of these Mughals? What do they mean to us? Why have you come all this way leading such a large force, in a struggle where we have no stakes? Whether it is the Emperor Shah Jahan or his son Dara, or for that matter, any of his other sons, what is it to us?

'We have eaten the emperor's salt, Maharaj. How can we breach the trust that he has placed in us?'

'Rubbish. These mlecchas are only using us for cannon fodder. Do you think that if the emperor triumphs or one of his sons seizes the throne, it will improve the condition of our people? They impose crippling taxes upon us only because we belong to a different faith and grind us down into the dust. Yes, perhaps at one time some of the high offices of state were open to those of our faith, but even that is no longer so, and certainly they do not treat us as their equals. Why shed blood for a cause that is not ours?'

Jaswant Singh was in a quandary. He was a Rajput, for whom a fate worse than death was reserved for those who broke their plighted word. He had never questioned his own loyalty to the empire, but the Brahmin was creating all sorts of doubts in his mind. In a way, what he was saying was nothing short of treason and people had been hanged for less. He could of course have the man thrown out of his camp, but such an insult to a Brahmin would not be countenanced by his troops, a large number of whom were Hindus. In any case, who had sent him here? Could he be one of Murad's men?

'Give us some time to think over the matter,' he said at length, deciding to dissemble. 'You know we will have to consult my commanders. If we suddenly give the orders to turn back, there might well be a revolt in our camp.'

'Think well about what I said,' replied the Brahmin, before leaving.

For the rest of that night, Jaswant pondered over his strange conversation with the Brahmin. Was this struggle really something which was of no concern to his people? Could he, in whom the emperor and Prince Dara had reposed such trust, just turn back and come away? Or was there something more sinister at play? He knew he had several enemies in court. Could this be a way of testing him, getting rid of him or at least ensuring that he was so disgraced that no more would any high office be offered to him or indeed to anyone of his race? Could Prince Dara himself be playing some deep game using him as a pawn? Try as he might he could find no answers to these conundrums, as he tossed and turned in his bed.

Next morning, just as Jaswant was completing his puja, Askaran and Askaran's junior staff officer, Danish Khan, sought immediate audience with him in his tent, bringing in tow a scout who had galloped all night evading Murad's patrols and whose foam flecked bay horse stood under a tree some distance away. The man himself could barely stand, but as he blurted out his tale, Jaswant's jaw tightened.

'Are you absolutely sure?' Jaswant asked.

'What I have seen is as clear to me as your exalted self standing before me, Excellency. My Lord Murad's troops swung south near the village of Kachraud, and when I came away to make my report they were barely ten kos from the encampment of Prince Aurangzeb,' replied the scout, regaining his breath.

'Could it not be some of Prince Murad's own advance

detachments?' asked Jaswant, still hoping against hope that what he was about to hear would not be true.

Through parched lips, the scout's face broke into a faint smile. 'The encampment is spread out over an enormous area, Excellency. No advance detachment would cover so much ground. Moreover I recognized Prince Aurangzeb's standards. It is none other than him and he has not less than 30,000 troops.'

'But how can that be?' asked Jaswant, still finding it difficult to accept what the scout was telling him. 'How could he cross the Narbada with such a large force, when all the ferries were guarded?'

'Prince Aurangzeb crossed the Narbada nearly forty kos upstream which was not guarded and where the water is less deep. Even so, he left some of his heavy guns behind, allowing them to catch up with him later lest it delay his advance. He then marched along the north bank of the river to rendezvous with Prince Murad at Kachraud as per their prior arrangement. That's what this man tells me,' said Askaran.

The scout nodded in confirmation.

'You were right Askaran,' said Jaswant, resignedly. 'We have been much too complacent. We thought we were confronted by a novice in the art of war with a handful of raw levies but we are now also facing a wolf with battle-hardened veterans, whose combined strength would well exceed our own. However, nothing is lost. The date and time and place of battle shall be of our own choosing, that is, if we cannot persuade the two Princes to withdraw. How many days march are their forces away from us?'

'About four days, Excellency.'

'Good. That will give us enough time to prepare for the battle. The exact time for commencement of hostilities will depend on the advice of the astrologers. Meanwhile, in accordance with the express desire of His Majesty, the Emperor and of Prince Dara, we shall address identical missives, both to Prince Murad and to Prince Aurangzeb to give up the idea of challenging the might of the empire and retire to their viceroyalties. After that we shall inspect some probable sites for the impending battle.'

Summoning a scribe, he cogitated on what to write for a long time, in the presence of Askaran and Danish, who would be witnesses if ever there was need to vouch for his efforts to get the two princes to withdraw. Then summoning up his courage he dictated the letters.

> *Your Highness,*
> *Your humble servant seeks your pardon for intruding upon your precious time, but the command of His Majesty, the Emperor, compels him to beseech you to eschew this fratricidal conflict and retire to your viceroyalty so that you may continue to enjoy his grace and beneficence. To this command, your humble servant adds his own entreaties. He has served the illustrious house of Timur for the last thirty-five years, and has fought for its glory from the snows of Herat to the steaming jungles of Bengal. Now, in the evening of his life, let him not be called upon to measure swords against a prince of the blood from that royal house. Rather, let him have the opportunity of rendering yet more service till the end of his days to the house of Timur so that its effulgence will illumine the entire earth and its lustre will eclipse even that of the sun and the moon.*

'Take these two messages and ride like the wind to the camps of my lords Aurangzeb and Murad and be sure to deliver them into their hands alone. We shall reward you with the revenues of a dozen villages if you accomplish the task successfully, but woe unto you if you fail,' he said handing the scrolls in two identical leather cases to his most intrepid horseman.

'I shall not fail you, Sire,' said the horseman as he swiftly mounted his steed, dug his spurs into its flanks and galloped forward.

'What do you think, Askaran? Will Aurangzeb and Murad retire from the conquest?'

'I doubt if they will,' the commander replied. 'They have come too far to retire now. Let us not forget that Prince Aurangzeb's ostensible purpose to come north is only to meet his father on knowing of the latter's illness, and which dutiful son would not do so.'

'Meet his father, indeed,' snorted Jaswant. 'With 30,000 picked troops? He is aiming for the empire of Hindustan, no less, but has devised a stratagem to conceal his moves by throwing dust in people's eyes. Perhaps the contents of my message, which he will receive by this evening, and the sight of our forces may induce him to have second thoughts. In any case, we have to prepare for the worst, and forcibly bar his further progress northward, so let us see which is the best terrain for doing so.'

Later that morning, he rode out from Ujjain, with Askaran, Danish, Raja Rai Singh Sisodia, Ifthikar Khan, Mukund Singh Hada and some other senior commanders, who would lead the imperial van. Jaswant took the great road running south, which Aurangzeb and Murad would have to travel, to debouch into the plains of Hindustan. Some distance south of Ujjain, the cultivated fields which supplied produce for the town, gave way to uneven ground criss-crossed with ruts and ditches, with swampy land to one side and a dry rivulet on the other. Away further to the south, obscured by low hills was the Narbada, meandering its way westward,which Aurangzeb had already crossed. Although the terrain was not entirely to his liking, Jaswant knew that this was the only chance of repelling the two rebellious princes, and if they were not held here, there would be no stopping them from striking at the very heart of the empire.

The party halted near the small village of Dharmat, as Jaswant surveyed the lay of the land.

'Well, what do you think of it?' Jaswant mused aloud, addressing no one in particular. The courtiers and generals knew when to speak and when to remain silent, but Danish, who knew well the time honoured battle plan in all such engagements which began with an artillery barrage closely followed by a massed cavalry charge ventured to blurt out his mind with all the impetuosity of youth.

'Lord, I would humbly submit that this would not be a suitable battlefield for the tactics generally employed to disperse the enemy. The ground presents a narrow front and is uneven, badly broken up, pitted and scarred. There will not be enough room for the cavalry to manouvere, thus rendering them quite ineffective.'

'What you say is not without sense, young man, but what other alternative do we have? Aurangzeb and Murad have already affected a junction and are marching northward, barely four days away. If we don't hold them here, and drive them back across the Narbada, what chance have we of holding them once they have crossed Ujjain? Indeed the same disadvantages we face will be faced by the rebels too. Did we not face similar terrain when we led His Majesty's armies in Subah-e-Tirhut?

There too we had the Ganges on one flank and marshy swampland on the other, and still we were successful.'

'Yes, my Lord,' interjected Askaran. 'But there His Majesty's enemies were poorly trained levies under a general who was practically insensible through opium. Here you are fighting a brilliant commander who does not know to retreat. Moreover he has a formidable artillery park manned by some firangees, who are excellent marksmen and will be able to pick on our massed cavalry with ease. I would strongly suggest that we choose more open ground where there will be ample scope to manouvere and outflank their artillery.'

'Where, Askaran? You tell us where. Allow the rebels deep into Hindustan and fight them north of Ujjain? What chance would we then have of forcing them back to their own viceroyalties? Remember my commission above all is to get them to return the way they came, by shedding as little blood as possible, and the deeper they enter into Hindustan, the more difficult the task will be. No, Askaran. We shall bar their way forward here. We trust they will choose not to precipitate matters, but if they decide to do so, we have no doubt that the impact of the shock cavalry charge by the Rathore and Hada squadrons will instill such fear in the hearts of these Deccanis that they will fly homewards. As for artillery, it may be good for destroying forts and demolishing walls but once one grapples with the enemy in close combat there is no force in the world that can resist the lance and the sword wielded by a Rajput.' Raja Rai Singh Sisodia and Mukund Singh Hada beamed with pleasure, when they heard these words from their chief.

Jaswant continued, 'In any case, as you can see, the terrain gets progressively worse for our cavalry, the further south we proceed. And whatever disadvantages we face will be faced by our opponents too. We will have to make do with the best of the situation and to turn it to our advantage we shall dig ditches on either sides of the battle field and flood them with water to prevent the enemy from outflanking us, and meanwhile our cavalry will push them against that adjoining swamp, by the side of which they must pass before debouching onto the battlefield.' Jaswant Singh pointed to a large patch of marshy land at some distance. 'Incidentally, before coming here we spoke to our pandit, who is also an astrologer. He predicted that the imperial troops will be victorious if hostilities commence at sunrise on the fourth day from today, which will give us good time to position ourselves here, if Aurangzeb and Murad are determined to press northward.' Fixing the accompanying generals and commanders with his keen eyes, he added, 'Let the baggage trains be brought up here and the disposition of the troops made in the usual formations so that we are in position well before evening, three days from today. There is not a moment to lose.'

Nine

WHEN AURANGZEB RECEIVED Jaswant Singh's message, a quiet smile of triumph broke on his lips. 'We have them,' he remarked quietly to Mahabat Khan, a close adviser. 'It is clear that Jaswant Singh is in two minds and does not know which way to turn. He is brave, but incapable of taking clear decisions and I forsee that will be his undoing.'

Aurangzeb had judged his opponent correctly, for Jaswant was truly on the horns of a dilemna. On the one hand was the commission given to him personally by the Emperor before he left Agra, to get the two princes to retire to their own viceroyalties, with as little bloodshed as possible. On the other hand there were the clear hints given by Dara to extirpate the rising threat from the south once and for all. And to add to it all were the doubts instilled in his mind by the Brahmin. What was he to do?

Sending for a scribe, Aurangzeb dictated the following reply:

Maharaja Saheb,

Would you deny us the opportunity of performing our filial duty by preventing us from paying our humble respects to our respected father, the Emperor of Hindustan, who lies seriously ill? Surely the Rajput code of filial obligations is not dead in Rathore veins. We have noted your contribution to the consolidation and spread of Mughal arms and your desire not to raise your sword against the house of Timur. These sentiments strike an answering chord in our own heart and if they be really sincere, come unescorted to Najabat Khan, who will take you to our son Mohammed Sultan, who in turn will then bring you to us for pardon, so that you may continue to serve us personally with the same loyalty you have displayed to the house of Timur in the past.

This message will certainly incense Jaswant Singh, thought Aurangzeb gleefully. As his Rajput pride would be pricked he would commit several errors in the battle that was now imminent. Sure enough, Aurangzeb had surmised correctly. When the rider bearing the message handed it to the Rathore commander, its condescending tone was too much for him to bear. How could he, the commander of the imperial armies, go and grovel before a man, even if he was a prince of the blood who was in open rebellion against the throne?

Jaswant was still smarting at the insult when dawn broke on the fourth day, and the two opposing armies came within sight of each other. Both armies were organized in the traditional order of battle with the artillery drawn up in a line in front and the vanguard behind them, with the two cavalry wings on either side of it and a little behind arrayed in echelons, the light cavalry in front and the heavy cavalry behind. Some distance behind the van stood the advanced reserve, which could go to the aid of the van or either flank if the need arose, and behind that was positioned the army commander on his elephant who occupied the centre with his view of the entire battlefield. Behind them was the rearguard and interspersed between these formations were the units of foot soldiers consisting of matchlock men, swordsmen, pikemen and archers.

It had rained intermittently throughout the night and the ruts and ditches of the uneven battlefield were now filled with water, but Jaswant Singh had no cause for alarm. He sat resplendent on his elephant at the centre of his vast army, confident that his tactics would win him victory, with Raja Rai Singh Sisodia surrounded by his clansmen leading the right wing, while Nawab Iftikhar Khan led the left. Likewise, Aurangzeb too was atop his elephant with Murad leading the right wing and Aurangzeb's younger son, Mohammed Azam, commanding the left. His elder son, Mohammed Sultan, was leading the van. At the precise moment, predicted by the pandit to be the most propitious, Jaswant opened hostitities with a fusillade of cannon and rocket fire at the advancing host, to which the response was not long in coming. As the distance shortened, with the opposing artillery firing at each other, the cavalry on both sides, their divisions one behind the other on that narrow front were taking up positions. When the imperial cavalry was in position, Jaswant ordered it to sweep forward and hit Aurangzeb's army in its flanks.

As they rode forward, first at a trot, then a canter and lastly at a gallop with lances levelled and swords flashing in the morning sunlight, the greater accuracy of the rebel artillery tore gaping holes in the imperial cavalry, but the horsemen quickly reformed and like a rushing tide they surged ahead.

'Prepare to receive cavalry!' the words rang out among Aurangzeb's front-line artillery commanders, as with their terrible war cry the first wave of the imperial horsemen, brushing aside the enemy fire, hurled themselves upon the opposing artillery. The impact of this first onslaught was tremendous. Swords flashed, lances were thrust, and many of the gunners who were busy loading their pieces after the first barrage were cut down in a welter of blood. Some of the guns were spiked, and the gunpowder stacked nearby was set on fire resulting in plumes of dense smoke billowing in the morning air and huge flames licking up into the sky. As the surviving gun crew abandoned their guns and sought to flee, the horsemen having pierced the artillery line now veered towards the van. Meanwhile, other horsemen echeloned behind them also surged ahead and lashed at the van. In the furious hand-to-hand combat that ensued, Aurangzeb's chief of artillery, Murshid Quli Khan, tried desperately to hold the fleeing gun crew back, but he received a mortal wound through a slashing sword. Pouring through the breached artillery line, the surging tide of imperial cavalry now supported by the foot soldiers rushing ahead, flung themselves at the van. Zulfiqar Khan, commander of the lead division of Aurangzeb's van, dismounted from his elephant and whirled his sword at the mounted imperial host but a well aimed spear thrust soon killed him.

Smelling victory in their nostrils, the imperial forces repeatedly hurled themselves at the van, hoping to breach it and scatter the rebels, thereby bringing the battle to an end. Indeed, for Aurangzeb the situation was becoming increasingly perilous. While Murad was valiantly repelling the sustained assaults of Iftikhar Khan who led the imperial left wing, and Mohammed Sultan was trying to hold the van together,

Aurangzeb noticed to his horror that his guns had been left without guards or gun crew and were unable to repel the further massed assaults of the imperial forces which were readying themselves to charge. Meanwhile, his van was on the verge of folding up on itself before the sustained surges of the imperial forces. Seeing that it was about to give way, Aurangzeb pushed forward the advanced reserve in its support but finding even that manouvere to be of little avail, he himself advanced forward with the household troops who were fanatically loyal to him. He momentarily succeeded in stabilizing the front, but not for long as the van seemed to be wilting under the enormous pressure. If the van was overwhelmed, Aurangzeb knew that nothing could save his army, for it would then be only moments before the imperial forces would reach the centre.

Is this the end? thought Aurangzeb grimly, as the battle raged in all its fury. *Have all our plans and efforts led only to this? Would Murad and we have to retreat with our tails between our legs and fly for our lives for having had the temerity to try colliding with the might of the Mughal empire*?

As the rebel forces were being pushed back and were ceding ground inch by bloody inch, on the repeated hammer blows of the imperial forces, Aurangzeb realized that only a miracle could save them.

Just at that moment, some of the gun crew who had fled at the ferocious assault by the imperial cavalry returned. Saif Shikan Khan, one of the most energetic of Aurangzeb's commanders, leapt down from his horse with sword in hand and ran to the nearest gunner, caught him by the scruff of the neck and dragged him to where an abandoned cannon stood with its balls and sacks of gunpowder stacked close by.

'Run away would you, you cowardly son of a whore?' he snarled, raising his sword as if about to smite him. He ground the terrified man's nose into the sack of gunpowder and then forced him to pour it down the barrel of the cannon. Seeing him, others in the gun crew sidled up, the cannon was loaded and the firing recommenced.

Meanwhile, the imperial forces, now believing that the field was theirs, had moved their van forward, followed by the advanced reserve and closely supported by Jaswant Singh who was himself leading the centre. But at the barrage of gunfire, fitful at first but increasingly sustained and aimed with pinpoint accuracy, their surging tide was stemmed and they began to reel and then recoil. The uneven terrain corrugated with ditches and potholes, now littered with the dead and the dying, impeded the rapid advance en masse of some of the rear units of the heavy cavalry which had been held back in reserve to deliver the coup de grâce. Those who got through the withering fire from the heavy guns and the lighter swivel pieces, and came within range, were picked off by the matchlock men and archers, with whom Auangzeb strengthened his front. Jaswant's strategem of digging ditches on either side of the battlefield and flooding it with water reduced the scope for the imperial forces to manouvere. The foreboding of young Danish Khan was proving tragically correct.

Those among the imperial shock cavalry who by sheer momentum were carried through the rebel van and even past it, now found their retreat cut off and without support, as Aurangzeb's men closed in upon them and fell upon them.

The tide of battle was beginning to turn against Jaswant Singh's forces.

Pushing forward with the centre, Aurangzeb waited for the

precise moment for the imperial thrust to falter.

'Now! Now! Move forward!' he ordered Shaikh Mir and Saif Shikan Khan, who commanded the two wings of his centre. They hit the imperial van on either flank with overwhelming force and the field was soon sodden with the blood of Rajput chivalry, including that of Mukund Singh Hada who had accompanied Jaswant Singh to the battlefield only four days earlier.

Seeing the attack of their van checked and then blunted, and the battle degenerated into a general scrimmage, disheartenment gradually spread among the imperial ranks. With little to hold them to the imperial cause, some of the Rajput chieftains at the edges of Jaswant Singh's right wing slid away from the melee, and with their followers prepared to return home, while units under Kasim Khan, which had so far not joined the battle, waiting to see which side would win, got ready to defect upon seeing the rebel hosts advancing towards them. Meanwhile, the centre commanded by Jaswant Singh himself and defended by his two thousand Rathore clanmen together with some Mughal formations held firm and Jaswant still hoped to snatch victory. But then Murad's divisions finding a gap in the ditches cut through his left wing and fell upon his camp.

'All is lost, Maharajah Saheb,' cried a mortally wounded Bundela warrior, one of the few who refused to captitulate as he rode upto Jaswant Singh's elephant, his sword arm slashed at the elbow and several deep sword cuts on his face and neck. 'Our flank has been turned. The enemy…has...plundered….our camp,' he managed to gasp, before tumbling lifeless from his horse, one foot still dangling from the stirrup.

Harried by Aurangzeb's artillery from the front, his right

wing weakened by desertions, and now outflanked to his left by Murad's divisions, Jaswant was facing his moment of truth. With dauntless courage, he had opposed the rebel forces without yielding. Despite two grievous wounds he had directed the movement of his troops with words of calm encouragement. Now the odds against him were overwhelming; to surrender to the enemy and beg for his life was to court eternal disgrace. Instead, what could be nobler than to hurl himself on the enemy at the head of his surviving Rathore clansmen and die the death of a heroic Rajput warrior, whose deed would be immortalized in song and legend by bards till the end of time?

'We have shown how a Rathore adheres to his plighted troth,' he cried above the tumult of the battle, as he prepared to descend from his elephant and mount a horse to lead the charge. 'The world shall now see that he is prepared to die in battle, for indeed what can be more glorious for a Rajput warrior than to charge at the enemy and die for his honour and his creed? Ask the commanders of the remaining formations to get ready to charge.'

As Jaswant placed his foot in the stirrup of the horse to mount, sheer weakness and exhaustion overcame him and he fell back. Two of his aides, Govardhan and Mahesh Das, who were standing close by, rushed to his help, gently placed him on the ground and moistened his lips with some water. 'No Maharajah Saheb, we will not let you throw away your precious life so uselessly. This battle may be lost but surely not the war,' said Govardhan. 'The empire will continue to need your services, and new armies can be raised against the rebels.'

'No, Govardhan, let me be true to my salt and my race,' Jaswant said, blood oozing out of his mouth as he made another effort to stand up and mount his horse.

'Mahesh Das ji, please convince Maharajah Saheb not to think of wasting his life in this fashion,' said Govardhan, in desperation.

Mahesh Das nodded vigourously in assent. 'Look at it in another way, Highness. This is basically a war between Mughal princes who are out to murder each other for their own private gain.Whether it is one prince who rules or the other,what is it to our people? Why should the head of the Rathores who traces his ancestry from the sun get himself involved in the domestic disputes of these Mughals, one of whom is no better than the other?

'But as the head of the imperial armies...' expostulated Jaswant Singh

Both Govardhan and Mahesh Das saw that Jaswant was now wavering a little and tried to press home the advantage as the battle still swirled around them.

'Exactly, Your Highness,'said Govardhan. 'As Commander you have a much greater responsibility than to throw your life away at the end of some Deccani spear. You can always raise a fresh army and you will have several opportunities to make the rebels taste the bitter draught of defeat. And what Mahesh Dasji says is absolutely correct. This struggle is really something between the Mughals and has nothing to do with our people.'

As the battle raged around him, Jaswant remembered the words of the Brahmin. Was this really his quarrel? Were Govardhan and Mahesh Das not making sense when they said that he may have lost the battle but not the war? Would it not be possible to hold the rebels at any one of the hundred places they would have to traverse before they reached the capital? And what about his own clansmen and the sacred soil of Jodhpur? Would they not require his counsel and his sword arm if any assault was made on its borders? Reluctantly, he gave up the idea of leading a charge and allowed himself to be led off the battlefield, along with the remnants of his clansmen, several of them as wounded as he was.

Amidst the din and the confusion of battle, Aurangzeb had been keeping a keen eye on the opposing commander on his elephant, while matching arrow with arrow and musket shot with musket shot, as his household troops threw a protective cordon around him repelling every effort made by the opposing horsemen to get close enough to strike at him. Then he saw Jaswant Singh who had alighted from his huge pachyderm, swaying near his horse, and being made to rest on the ground as his warriors formed a ring around him. Had he finally prevailed? When he saw Jaswant's horse being led away from the battlefield with the commander himself lurching in the saddle, clutching his side, surrounded by a few faithful retainers, he needed no further confirmation. A great sigh of relief coursed through him.

Waving his sword aloft in the air, so that all could see, he cried out aloud, 'Allah be praised. The road to Hindustan is open.'

Ten

The starless night was hot and still. Dara and savants from different faiths, reclining on silk-covered bolsters, fanned by attendants, sat on the terrace of Agra Fort, engaged in one of the heir-apparent's favourite occupations—finding a common meeting ground for all religions through discussions and debate. Just then there was commotion at the far end of the terrace. An attendant ran forward and then swiftly returned to where Dara and the others were seated.

'A courier has come from Maharaja Jaswant Singh, Sire. He says he bears a very important despatch, to be delivered to Lord Dara Shukoh personally.'

'Bring him here.' Doubtless he was bringing good tidings, thought Dara.

The attendant returned with the courier, who was accompanied by some palace guards carrying flaming torches. The man had to be practically propped up as he dug into his torn, dirty, travel-stained tunic and drew out a thin cylinder. Opening its lid, Dara took out a tightly wrapped parchment. As he ran his eyes over its contents by the light of the torches, his elation turned to horror.

'We wish to be left alone,' he said curtly.

All those in the gathering got up and left silently, seeing the taut expression on Dara's face, and only the attendants, the courier and the palace guards were left as he went through the contents of the despatch again, this time more slowly. Sent immediately after the battle, which had been fought eight days earlier, the courier had ridden practically non-stop, breaking journey only to change mounts.

'...Aurangzeb had crossed the Narbada with some 30,000 troops...effected junction with Murad's 10,000...imperial forces defeated at Dharmat near Ujjain...several high-ranking imperial officers, including Iftikar Khan, and Rajput noblemen slain.... imperial baggage train in rebel hands along with the artillery, tents, pack animals and treasure...the two princes now heading north towards Dholpur to cross Chambal river before pressing on to Agra...'

'You took part in the battle, did you not?' asked Dara.

The rider nodded glumly.

'Tell us all that you saw,' said Dara earnestly. A low stool was brought on which he sat opposite the rider.

As the man seemed to be choking on his first few words, Dara politely said, 'Collect yourself, think well and then recount to us all that happened. What is your name?'

'Bahadur Singh,' said the rider, who by now had steadied himself. In short, staccato sentences, he described all that he had seen and heard, right from the initial exchange of artillery by the opposing forces, till the plundering of the imperial camp by Aurangzeb's men.

Dara listened in silence. Only now and then did he put in a short, probing question to elicit further information. One thought was uppermost in his mind. Had Jaswant Singh resisted firmly enough or had he thrown in the towel a little too early? He had to have an answer to the question, for he remembered that the emperor had wanted Nawab Kasim Khan to lead the imperial troops.

'And what happened to Maharajah Saheb?' asked Dara delicately.

The rider looked Dara in the eye, his shoulders stiffening. He replied in a measured tone, 'He fought till the end with all the proud valour of our race. Despite being grievously wounded, he was preparing to lead a charge at the enemy, but he nearly fainted from loss of blood and was dissuaded only with the greatest difficulty from throwing away his life uselessly.'

'What about Nawab Kasim Khan? Surely he would have put up a stout defence?' asked Dara. Kasim Khan had been paid out of the imperial treasury for raising three new divisions, and had boasted to Dara that he would have Aurangzeb and Murad scuttling back to their viceroyalties if they ever dared to venture out of it, or he would return with their heads and throw them at the heir-apparent's feet.

The honest soldier remained silent.

'Don't hesitate, and tell us. Say what you have to say,' said Dara, impatiently.

'My Lord, I'm a common man. How can I speak about a man as exalted as Nawab Saheb? But it's God's truth, Sire, that he kept his forces away from the battle despite repeated directions from Maharajah saheb to engage the enemy, and when he saw the opposing army approaching, he fled with all his divisions.'

Dara'slips curled in disgust. Was there no end to cowardice

and treachery? His brain was in a whirl, for a hundred things now needed to be done. He forced himself to think calmly. A fresh army would have to be raised, provisioned, equipped and rushed to Dholpur to bar Aurangzeb's advance across the Chambal. Fortifications would have to be raised along its banks, and sufficient reserves would need to be kept in Agra. Sulaiman would have to give up the fruitless chase for Shuja and be immediately recalled.

'Have this man attended to and see that he lacks nothing,' Dara barked to one aide, nodding towards the rider. Summoning another, he said, 'Inform Paymaster General Askar Khan, and Khallilullah Khan, as well as Commanders Firuz Jang, Sayyid Bahir Hussain, Zafar Khan, Fakhar Khan, Chhatrasal Singh Hada, Diler Beg and Rustam Noor that we wish to confer with them at first light tomorrow.'

The next day, at the appointed hour, the noblemen entered Dara's private audience chamber.

'We have summoned you,' began Dara 'because we are informed that our brothers Aurangzeb and Murad, having crossed the Narbada, have defeated our forces under Maharaja Jaswant Singh near Ujjain eight days ago. They are now marching northwards towards Dholpur, where they propose to cross the Chambal river to strike at us here, in Agra. It is the Emperor's firm decision that they be prevented from crossing the Chambal at Dholpur, because from that point onwards there is no natural barrier of which we can take advantage. If we fail to hold them there, we will have to fight them at the gates of Agra. Each of you will now present the figures of the actual muster roll under your command and your additional requirements to bring your forces up to full strength. Each horseman who participates in the campaign with his horse and weapon will receive a gold mohur and a foot soldier will receive five silver pieces. Muskets and other weaponry will be provided by the head of the imperial ordnance.' Dara looked at Nawab Zafar Khan, who nodded. 'An inventory should be taken of the number of serviceable elephants and camels and also of the heavy and medium guns and swivel pieces.'

As words tumbled out of Dara, the thin, taciturn Nawab Firuz Jang, head of the Afghan Sayyids and arguably the ablest of the imperial commanders, cast a measuring eye on the heir-apparent. He noticed the weak irresolute mouth, the soft pudgy hands more used to flipping through a book than grasping the hilt of a sword. Was this prince planning to measure swords against his dour, flint-like younger brother?

Wisely he held his peace but Zafar Khan, one of the senior-most commanders, suggested, 'Sire, as this dispute is at best a family quarrel, might it not be a better idea for Prince Aurangzeb and Prince Murad to be allowed to present themselves before the Emperor? The Emperor, by the sheer effulgence of his personality, is bound to chasten the two, who will then retire to their viceroyalties without any shedding of the imperial blood.'

Dara's lips twisted in a sneer. 'We have not convened this conference to hear this kind of defeatist nonsense. Why, Khan Saheb, have your years on earth made you take leave of your senses or is it sheer cowardice that prompts you to make such a ridiculous suggestion? The only way in which Aurangzeb and Murad will be presented before the Emperor is with chains around their necks, unless of course the two decide to run back to their viceroyalties at the sight of the imperial forces, and for that, young Chhatrasal Hada here should be enough.'

There was stunned silence in the room. If anyone else had

offered such a mortal insult, the Nawab would have drawn his sword, but it came from the Prince of the blood, the heir-apparent to the throne, and Zafar Khan's unswerving oath of fealty to the Emperor held him back. He said nothing and as the conference concluded, the participants filed out, avoiding meeting his eye.

The next few days passed in a flurry of activity. Old cannons were made serviceable, their carriages oiled and greased and the barrels of new ones cast; muskets were repaired; stores of ball and shot and gunpowder were replenished; elephants, camels and horses were readied for the campaign; fresh levies were raised, equipped and given a modicum of training; rations were commandeered in case the campaign lasted longer than expected, and a hundred other things were attended to, in what all knew would be the coming struggle for the mastery of Hindustan.

It was estimated that it would take at least five weeks for the rebel forces to reach Dholpur. Accordingly it was decided that advance elements of the imperial army would proceed towards Dholpur immediately and after seizing all the ferries and crossing points, position the artillery over the banks of the River Chambal to frustrate any attempt to ford it, while Dara with the main body of the army would follow and reach Dholpur ten days later to repel the advance of Aurangzeb's army.

Meanwhile, arguments raged between father and son in those long hot summer nights. Shah Jahan still believed that the matter could be settled, if only his four sons could sit together in his presence and sort out their differences.

'We are convinced that only disgrace will befall the house of Timur, if this fratricidal conflict is allowed to drag on any longer,' the Emperor told Dara. 'We have conferred with several nobles whose advice we value, and all of them feel that if Aurangzeb and Murad were to come here and see us they would be satisfied that we are fully recovered and are not being held under any duress, and they would return to their viceroyalties.'

'Well, that is the ostensible purpose of their visit,' remarked Dara, looking out of the window. 'They say they are only performing their filial duty by coming to visit their ailing father, but Aurangzeb comes with 30,000 picked veterans at his back and with Murad in his tow. Some peaceful visit it seems!

'How can I convince you, Sire? All this demonstration of affection is only a ruse. Aurangzeb wants nothing less than the empire of Hindustan, even when you, Sire, are alive, and he will stop at nothing to achieve his ambition. If he had really wanted to come to see you, surely he could have done that accompanied by a few retainers instead of bringing such a huge army.'

'Probably he was worried that you may bar his way, or that some rajas on his route northwards may pose obstacles. Remember some tracts in that region are not fully pacified.'

'But 30,000 troops, Sire! War elephants, siege guns, cavalry, foot soldiers. And Murad with his own contingents of troops. All this can only mean one thing—war! Well, if they want a war, they shall have it. Ever since we were young boys, I have noticed this possessive streak in Aurangzeb, wanting to grasp anything someone else had; and once he had it, not willing to let go of it. He and Murad have defeated one of our armies, but the empire of Hindustan is one prize Aurangzeb is not going to get merely because he wants it. As long as there is breath left in my body, I will defend your right, Sire, to decide who in time will sit on the throne. If it is your wish that the empire should go to Aurangzeb, or you wish to make any other arrangment, this humble son of yours will accept it willingly, but I shall not allow it to be wrested at the point of a sword.'

Soon the appointed day for the advance elements of the imperial army to proceed towards Dholpur arrived. 'Remember we want all the ferries and crossing points on the Chambal at Dholpur, on either side of the river for a distance of ten kos seized, and gun emplacements positioned on the high banks to prevent any attempt at crossing,' said Dara. He cautioned Fakhar Khan, the commander of the advance regiments, 'There must be patrolling of the river near Dholpur night and day, and any suspicious-looking person should be immediately apprehended and detained, till we arrive and decide what to do with him. Send regular reports of your progress. Above all there should be no repetition of what happened at Dharmat. We shall follow with the main body of the army just one watch after dawn exactly ten days from today, which the court astrologers have pronounced to be the most auspicious for any campaign in a southern direction.'

'Your orders will be followed meticulously, Sire,' replied Fakhar Khan. 'This humble servant of yours will not fail the empire.' Saluting Dara courteously, he leapt onto his charger and spurred it forward to the head of the leading units. As drums beat and banners waved gaily, the army streamed out of Agra bound for Dholpur.

The night before Dara's own departure for Dholpur, a full moon beamed down on Agra. Dara lay with his wife Nadira Begum and drew her tenderly towards him. 'You are even more beautiful now than when we got married over a quarter of a century ago,' he said, looking wonderingly into her eyes, fondling a wisp of a curl that fringed her forehead, now touched with the slightest tinge of grey.

'You flatterer,' she whispered back. 'Only you can see any beauty in an old hag like me, when there are several ones far younger and more attractive than me among my own maids in waiting, any of whom are yours only for the asking.'

'No dearest. For me it has always been you and you alone. So shall it be till the end of my days.'

'Sssshhhhhhh...Don't speak of such inauspicious things as your days ending. You are destined to be the emperor of Hindustan, and after us our progeny shall reign for as many years as there are stars in the sky,' she said in a low voice. Then holding his face close to her own and staring intently into his eyes, she said, 'You will be careful, my lord, if you have to battle against your brothers, won't you? And you will see that Siphir comes to no harm, won't you? By God's grace, victory has crowned Sulaiman's efforts against your brother Shuja, but we are very worried about Siphir as he has not been tested in any big battle till now. According to court gossip, Murad is brave as a lion, but a fool with little knowledge of tactics in warfare. It is Aurangzeb who has to be watched for he is crafty, shrewd and a master tactician. He can go to any length he deems appropriate, to gain what he desires.'

Dara laughed and said, 'Don't you worry your pretty little head, my dearest. The sight of the imperial army itself will be enough to send that absurd imposter scampering back with his tail between his legs. And if it comes to a battle, why, the whole affair should be over in a couple of hours. Siphir will command the left wing of the battle order, and if there has to be any engagement, he will acquit himself boldly like the young tiger that he is. After all, he is our son.'

'We only wish to God what you say comes true,' she murmured, as some vague premonition of a looming disaster was forming in her mind. Then, wishing to dispel the gloom that seemed to be enveloping her despite the fullness of the moon, she asked, 'You know dearest, what we cherish most among all the gifts you have given us in the quarter century of our married life?'

'What?' he asked.

She got up and went to a trunk and, rummaging in it, brought out an album. 'This,' she said. She opened its flyleaf. By the light of the moonbeams he read, 'This album was presented to his nearest and dearest companion, the lady Nadira Begum, by Prince Dara Shukoh, son of the Emperor Shah Jahan.'

'You mean, you have kept this all these years?' he asked in wonderment.

She nodded happily. 'What are diamonds and pearls, when this album bears our Lord's own handwriting in his beautiful Nastaliq script?'

'Indeed we are blessed to have been favoured with a wife like you,' he said, as she snuggled against him, and both waited for the dawn to break.

Well before the sun was grazing the tops of the distant trees towards the east underneath a cloudless sky, Dara's army, with banners unfurled, great kettle drums beating, and trumpets blaring, marched out of the gates of Agra fort towards Dholpur.

Eleven

'Absurd! Impossible! We refuse to believe it,' said Dara furiously, as a contrite Fakhar Khan and other commanders stood before him at Dholpur with their hands crossed before them, and heads bowed, not daring to look up at him. 'We had given clear instructions to you, Khan Saheb, that all the ferries and crossing points at this place and ten kos on either side of it should be guarded, and any attempt made by our brothers to cross the Chambal here should be foiled till we ourselves arrived to take stock of the situation. Why were our commands disobeyed? Don't you know the penalty for disobeying imperial orders?'

'Sire, your orders were meticulously obeyed,' replied Fakhar Khan nervously, through parched lips. 'As soon as the units reached here, we seized all the ferries and mounted cannon at all the crossing points, on either side up to a distance of ten kos as directed. Round-the-clock patrolling on foot and on horseback was introduced, spies were sent out to watch and report on enemy movements and my commanders can vouch for the fact that not even a rat could have got past the arrangements that had been made.'

'Then how did they cross the Chambal?' Dara asked derisively. 'Did they grow wings? Did some heavenly angels transport them through the air, elephants, camels, cavalry, heavy guns, soldiers in their thousands, all unseen by mere mortals?'

Fakhar Khan ignored the jibe. 'The enemy did not come anywhere near Dholpur at all, Sire. They by-passed Dholpur altogether and marched by way of Gwalior. A zamindar of that pargana for the promise of a huge reward told them of a little-used ford several kos east of Dholpur, with practically no water in it at this time of the year. The enemy, by a series of forced marches, reached that spot and got his advance units and the bulk of his artillery across followed by the rest of the army.'

'Rest assured we shall get to the bottom of this,' Dara said ominously. 'And if we suspect the least hint of treachery in allowing our brothers to cross the Chambal unimpeded, the person responsible will be made to pay for it with his head. Now in the face of this unprecedented situation, we shall confer with our senior-most commanders and take counsel as to our future course of action, while the others may leave.'

When only the half-dozen or so senior-most commanders were left in Dara's presence, he turned to Firuz Jang and said, 'Well, Nawab Saheb, we have no alternative but to fall back on Agra, isn't it?'

'No, Sire,' the doughty warror replied tersely.

Indeed, the position of the imperial army had been rendered extremely precarious. Aurangzeb and Murad had completely outflanked their opponents and were heading towards the Mughal capital, which was barely five days' march away, with no force in sight to stop them, as Dara and his troops were all gathered around Dholpur. The elaborate arrangements made to prevent Aurangzeb crossing the Chambal had been rendered useless. Sulaiman Shukoh with divisions of the imperial forces was still three weeks' marching distance from Agra and wouldn't be able to provide any help. Aurangzeb would now have to be fought and defeated at the very gates of that city with whatever forces Dara could muster.

It was decided that the imperial forces break camp immediately and return by the quickest means to Agra for its defence. The decision was put speedily into execution. The gun emplacements along the banks of the River Chambal were demolished; the entrenchments were broken; the bivouacs were brought down; the tents and pavilions were dismantled; the elephants, horses, camels and mules were harnessed and loaded; the troopers who were looking forward to a much-needed rest were roused and made ready to march back; and slowly the huge, lumbering army picked itself up and started retracing the steps by which it had come.

Dara was in a fever of impatience to get back. Several of the heavier pieces of artillery that sat embedded on the river riverbank had to be abandoned and the forced marches each day in the blistering heat, at the height of the north Indian summer, through waterless tracts took their toll, but on the fifh day of their departure from Dholpur, advance scouts of the imperial army approaching Agra from the southwest saw, as if in a mirage, the marble dome of the Taj Mahal shimmering in the distance.

Meanwhile, Aurangzeb had not been idle. Impelled by his implacable will, his forces allied to those of Murad had advanced northwards after crossing the River Chambal near Gwalior and approached the banks of the River Jumna, to the east of Agra, at about the same time as Dara's army was approaching it from the southwest.

In its journey eastwards, some four kos past the Agra Fort, the River Jumna swept northward in a great arc before straightening out again. A few kos south of the bend lay the village of Samugarh and further south as well as to the east of it, stretched a wide featureless plain, distinguished by only babool trees.

'This will be the most suitable site to offer battle,' advised Chhatrasal Hada, the commander of the Rajput cavalry, and Firuz Jang, as they approached the plain, reconnoitering the area for the best place to make their stand. 'The enemy will have to pass this way to reach Agra. In numbers we are far superior and unlike at Dharmat, the ground is hard and crisp, with plenty of room to manouvere. As soon as the rebels are sighted the cavalry will swoop in from either side, in successive waves, sever its van from the rest of the army and make for its centre where Aurangzeb is sure to be. Once we reach him, the battle will be over in a manner of minutes.'

'We agree,' said Dara, as he hastened forward with the army. Skirting the fort of Agra which lay to his left, Dara dropped camp at a convenient spot on the edge of the plain with a view to occupy whatever vantage points the site offered. That night, the campfires of Dara's army were spread out over the plain, twinkling like so many stars in the sky.

Night gave way to the dawn of another blisteringly hot morning, and as scouts brought news of the approaching army of Aurangzeb, Dara too ordered his forces to march forward in full panoply as he sat on his enormous elephant which was plated with steel, with knives and swords lashed to its trunk, while the sunlight glinted on his shining breastplate. Excitement rose fever pitch in the imperial ranks, who were convinced that the mere sight of their standards and their banners, together with their sheer numbers, would make the Deccani rabble turn tail and run.

Suddenly, inexplicably, when the opposing armies were within sight of each other, Dara called a halt. Consternation spread among his leading commanders. 'Halt? Now?' thought Chhatrasal Singh Hada, as he galloped up to Dara.

'This is no time to halt, Sire. Give the orders for hostitilties to commence. The enemy has trudged throughout the night to reach the battlefield and is completely exhausted. Many of their units have not even arrived. No better time can there be than this to launch the attack. Let the enemy be initially softened by a few artillery barrages and then I shall lead my cavalry onto him. The field will be ours within the hour. Please, Sire, do not delay. Every moment lengthens the odds.'

Diler Khan and Sayyid Bahir Khan, who were within earshot, also weighed in. 'What the Rajput chieftain says is absolutely correct, Sire. If we lose this opportunity we may not get another. The enemy is weak and dispirited at the moment. One resolute charge and the battle will be won.'

'We value your advice, but before departing we had sworn an oath to the Emperor that if we ever came face to face with our brothers on the battlefield, we would not be the first to open hostilities. Yes, if he makes the first hostile move, we will reply with full force, but we still retain the hope that the sight of the imperial standards will make them see reason…'

'Sire, we are losing precious time,' said Firuz Jang, who had also ridden up to where the generals were conferring with Dara. 'This is not the occasion to hesitate. Your enemy stands before you. His intentions are clear. He has no intention of withdrawing and every moment adds to his strength as he brings up his forces. If we do not act now, the sceptre may well be wrested from your grasp!'

'Let us wait a little longer, till we know what exactly Aurangzeb's intentions are. Meanwhile, all of you retain your positions,' said Dara prevaricatingly.

As the Commanders returned to their given stations, baffled by this attitude of their leader, which many ascribed to sheer pusillanimity, dissension began to creep into the imperial ranks. Even otherwise beneath a superficial unity, jealousy and lack of cooperation had characterized the relations between the different units of the imperial army and now, these antagonisms and suspicions further simmered. Had there been some secret understanding with Aurangzeb? Did Dara propose to sell out? All sorts of dark rumours began to circulate among the troops, which by slow degrees sapped their will to fight. As the morning wore on and the sun blazed down on Dara's troops, with unrelenting fury, a fierce loo added to their travails. Clad in their heavy steel armour, standing at their positions hour after hour under the pitless sun, several troopers collapsed, unable to move even a step.

The respite that Aurangzeb had gained through Dara's indecision was employed usefully by him in hurrying his forces onto the battlefield. Learning that Dara had halted his forces he muttered a silent prayer to Allah, and dismounting from his elephant and jumping on to a horse, he galloped to where his artillery commander Saif Shikan Khan stood, some distance behind the rest of the army with his shoulder to the wheel of a gun carriage that had got stuck in a rut, setting a personal example to the gun crew. 'Shabash Nawab Saheb!' cried Aurangzeb. 'With commanders like you, we cannot lose!

Never was there greater need for your guns. Let them add one more glorious chapter in the annals of war. The future of the Mughal empire now rests in your hands. Let it not be ruled by an apostate, who brings nothing but disgrace to the true faith.'

Riding tirelessly up and down, unmindful of the wilting heat, Aurangzeb got the bulk of his army near the approaches to the battlefield by the late afternoon. As the sun finally set, Dara's army retired, bewildered at the total lack of action when they had the enemy at their mercy. Aurangzeb's forces bivouaced for the night, earning a much-needed rest, as they prepared for the morrow's battle. That night, addressing his generals, Aurangzeb exhorted them to show their mettle by their bravery.

'We have traversed a great distance,' he said, 'and the morrow must show that the effort has not been in vain. Let the word go forth that tomorrow is the day of valour. With inflexible resolve you must smite the enemy, such that the records of the office of fortune resound with your deeds of bravery.'

Well before dawn the next day, the opposing armies were readying themselves for the coming battle. Each of their squadrons were taking up their battle positions, and within two hours of daybreak, Aurangzeb, with his cohorts marshalled and his ranks dressed, was ready to advance. Murad was commanding the left wing, while Dara's forces were prepared to receive the assault. Amidst the boom of the great war drums, interspersed with the staccato beat of the smaller, lighter kettle drums, the blaring of trumpets and pipes, the trumpeting of elephants, the neighing of horses and the creaking of the artillery wheels, mixed with hundreds of other sounds, the two huge unwieldy armies approached each other from opposite ends of the battlefield, and well before the sun had reached its zenith, the imperial forces could sight the standards and penants of the rebels.

As the intervening distance shortened, a gunner from Aurangzeb's artillery, perhaps seeking to find the correct range, fired a shot. The cannon ball ploughed harmlessly into the ground, far short of the imperial front, but any inhibitions Dara had were now overborne. Aurangzeb had fired the first shot and Dara was no longer bound by his oath to the Emperor. His battle plan was simple—soften the enemy front with artillery fire, overwhelm the rebel van through successive cavalry attacks and then strike at the rebel centre where Aurangzeb was sure to be. With Aurangzeb killed or captured, the rebellion would collapse in a matter of hours.

'Yes!' cried Dara atop his elephant when his Chief of Artillery sought permission to respond. Thereupon, the imperial artillery which was positioned all along the front, set up a sustained barrage. When the smoke from the batteries cleared, finding little or no response from the enemy Dara thought the battle was as good as won, as his opponents had taken fright and all that was now required was a little mopping up. He did not realize that the shelling had been far short of range and had done very little damage. Aurangzeb was wisely conserving his ammunition till his opponents were at closer quarters.

With a great sweep of his arm, Dara then signalled to Rustam Khan, who commanded the left wing of the imperial cavalry, to lead the charge. Levelling their lances and with swords drawn and glinting in the sunlight, Rustam Khan's horsemen yelling blood-curdling war cries swept through the gaps between the guns and fell upon Aurangzeb's right wing.

Saif Shikan Khan was waiting for them. Volley after volley of well-directed artillery fire rang out, supported by a hail of arrows, bullets and javelins from the foot soldiers that stood close by, which checked the momentum of the charge. Wave upon wave of horsemen hurled themselves on Aurangzeb's right, but the line did not break. Baffled by the resistance, the cavalry veered towards Aurangzeb's van commanded by Mohammed Sultan. Desperate hand-to-hand fighting now ensued and the right flank of his van was in danger of being overwhelmed by sheer force of numbers, when reinforcements from the advanced reserve arrived and scattered Rustam Khan's men, who fell back under Siphir Shukoh.

Despite the reverses suffered by his left wing, the battle was not going badly for Dara. To his right, the Uzbek contingents under Khallilullah Khan had advanced under a hail of arrows to meet the injudicious thrust of Aurangzeb's left wing commanded by Murad, who without waiting for Aurangzeb's orders had advanced forward to grapple with his sworn enemy Chatrasal Singh Hada who led Dara's van. Finding a gap created between Aurangzeb's artillery and Murad's divisions, the imperial cavalry led by Chhatrasal Singh Hada and other Rajput noblemen charged forward to exploit it. Clad in robes of saffron, the colour of sacrifice, the horsemen, heavily armed with swords and lances, cut their way right up to Murad's elephant, confident that the rebel artillery could not molest them without killing their own men.

'You dare dispute the throne with Dara Shukoh?' cried Raja Rup Singh Rathore, shouting to the mahout to make Murad's elephant kneel, as he flung a spear at the rebel prince, which grazed his arm. The other warriors swarmed around the towering beast, firing a hail of arrows and soon Murad's howdah resembled the back of a porcupine. Murad himself suffered three wounds on his face and his mahout was killed, but he did not flinch and fought with all the courage for which he was renowned. The ground around the feet of his elephant was littered with the bodies of the Rajput warriors in their saffron tunics, mingling with the blood of his own men. An arrow from his bow brought down Rup Singh, with a chaplet of pearls still tied to his turban, but the Rajputs, now reinforced by other units of Dara's army, had shifted their focus on to Aurangzeb.

Seeing Murad in danger of being overwhelmed, Aurangzeb had rushed to the aid of his brother and the imperial forces now hacked their way up to Aurangzeb himself. Lashing the feet of his elephant together with iron chains, so that it would not bolt, Aurangzeb atop his howdah, cool, undaunted, instilled fresh heart amongst the elite corps of veterans who guarded his person.

'Khuda hai! Khuda hai!' he cried. 'We shall conquer or die here, for this is our Deccan. There shall be no retreat. If we triumph, which no doubt we shall, all the treasures of Hindustan will be at your feet, but if we die, our heads will rest on our sabres in paradise!'

Blow for blow, steel for steel, the two armies were locked in a close combat, which was unparalled in its ferocity. Time and again the imperial forces led by Chatrasal Singh Hada, who had dismounted from his elephant and mounted a horse, tried to reach up to Aurangzeb and deliver a mortal blow, but each time they were thwarted. A Rajput paladin dismounting from his horse, and hacking his way up to the elephant through a welter of blood, tried to sever the howdah's girth so that Aurangzeb would come crashing down, but even this act of supreme bravery was of little avail as a burly guardsman cut him down and others were about to decapitate him, when Aurangzeb, who recognized courage when he saw it, shouted to them to desist from doing so.

Thoroughly exhausted, maddened with thirst, their ranks grieviously thinned by the repeated attacks on that ring of steel around Aurangzeb, which showed no signs of breaking, the flowers of Rajput chivalry, including Chhatrasal Singh Hada and several others, had fallen by the late afternoon, and the assaults by Dara's right wing had begun to falter. But Aurangzeb still sat upon his elephant, serving as a rallying point for his forces, as did Murad.

Meanwhile, Dara, thinking that Rustam Khan's charge had succeeded, moved from his position in the centre towards his left to envelop the enemy, but met with such a sustained barrage from Aurangzeb's artillery that many of his supporting troops scattered. Then, enthused by the news that at the other end of the battlefield the imperial cavalry had reached up to Aurangzeb's elephant and were trying to break the cordon of steel around him, Dara swung to his right, intending to engage Aurangzeb from his side and bring the battle to an end. For a time the momentum of his advance carried him between Aurangzeb and his lead divisions, who had rushed so many men forward that his own guards were sorely depleted. At that moment, one determined thrust by Dara towards his hated brother, one spasm of resolve and victory might still have been his, but that was not to be. Sheer exhaustion overcame him and he called a halt. The moment passed, the momentum was lost.

Worse for Dara, by these manoeuvres he had traversed practically the entire length of his front, not only blocking his artillery from responding to enemy fire for fear of hitting their own men, but exposing his left flank to withering volleys from Aurangzeb's batteries. More importantly it had lost him an overview of how the battle was developing and control of his forces over the entire battlefield. By the time he realized his folly and called up his artillery it was too late. Most of the gun crew had fled, or were engaged in looting his own camp. As the remnants of Dara's divisions fell back, the burning sun, the terrible heat, the swirling dust, the absence of even a drop of water and the deadly accuracy of Aurangzeb's artillery were taking their grim toll.

As the evening shadows lengthened, it was evident that the end was near. His left wing repulsed, his right wing mauled, his van and centre in disarray, Dara still courageously tried to recover. He disposed the troops that remained with him as best as he could, with words of encouragement, as he waited for the onslaught which was not long in coming. Advancing on a broad front, with his artillery blazing, confident that there would be little or no reply, Aurangzeb concentrated the attack on Dara. As the cannon balls and rockets fell amidst Dara and his entourage, Khallilullah Khan rode up to him.

'Dismount from your elephant, Sire, and take to a horse,' he cried above the din of battle. 'You will then be able to move more easily among your troops who will rally around you. Otherwise the imperial cause is lost.'

Foolishly, Dara did just that. Bruised, beaten, battered, bone-weary and parched with thirst, more dead than alive, the remnants of Dara's troops looked around and found his howdah empty. Aurangzeb could be clearly seen, seated on his elephant advancing towards them. Murad too was conspicuous on his elephant, by Aurangzeb's side. But where was Dara? Consternation spread amongst his troops. Had he been killed?

Had he deserted the Emperor's cause? Why fight for a cause and risk one's life uselessly when the principal exemplar of that cause himself was nowhere to be seen to defend it, or probably worse, had sold out to the enemy? Questions turned into doubts, and doubts into panic. As it is there was little to hold this disparate force together and many units were looking for a suitable opportunity to flee. With Dara's howdah empty, they waited no longer. The defeat became a rout and the imperial army dissolved like a snowball in the summer sun.

Late that night, a handful of men in the terminal stages of physical exhaustion, broken in mind and spirit, were challenged by the guards when they crept furtively up to the gates of Agra fort and sought admittance. It was Dara, the anointed heir to the Mughal empire, with his son Siphir and a few of his most loyal followers, fleeing after their defeat on the plains of Samugarh.

Twelve

'AH! WELCOME, ESTEEMED brother,' said Aurangzeb as the heralds announced the arrival of Prince Murad. Aurangzeb rose from the masnad and advanced to the entrance of the red-carpeted shamiana, arms outstretched to hug the burly figure of his younger brother, whom he had invited to discuss future arrangements, whose own guards fell back when their master entered the marquee.

It was a little over three weeks after the battle of Samugarh. Agra, along with Delhi, were now Aurangzeb's, and his father was a prisoner, confined to his apartments overlooking the Taj Mahal. Dara was a fugitive, who had escaped with his wife, his son Siphir and a ragtag bunch of devoted followers from Agra to Delhi and thence onto Lahore, pursued by Nasiri Khan, who had switched sides after the Battle of Dharmat and pledged his allegiance to the rising star, boasting that he would bring Dara and throw him at his master's feet. Shuja was still far away in Bengal, licking his wounds after his defeat by Sulaiman, and Aurangzeb seemed to be the monarch of all that he surveyed.

The only thorn in Aurangzeb's flesh was his brother

Murad. He proposed to pull out that thorn, choosing the occasion to do so when Murad was camping at Rupnagar near Mathura on a tiger hunt, while Aurangzeb himself was on his way from Agra to Delhi and their respective camps were only a few kos apart.

Aurangzeb's camp was located in a large clearing, which had been fenced off with stout bamboo poles arranged in concentric circles, with tight security by his household troops. The marquee stood in the centre of the clearing, surrounded by Aurangzeb's tents and that of his principal officers. It was shut out from prying eyes by thick draperies, but a portion of it was open to the skies. It was strewn with priceless carpets, and at one of its ends, placed on a slightly raised platform, stood the masnad, covered with the finest silk, and bolsters all around. A low table stood in front of the masnad while diaphanous curtains at the single point of entry into the marquee rustled lightly in the gentle breeze that had struck up a few hours earlier.

'So, what do you have in mind, brother?' began Murad almost immediately after he had unbuckled his sword, put it to one side, eased his considerable bulk onto the masnad and adjusted a bolster to make himself more comfortable. There was a hint of truculence in his voice.

'There will be time enough for that. We have the whole evening before us,' replied Aurangzeb smoothly. 'Tell us, have your wounds healed? Let us see them.' He lifted a lamp and brought it close to Murad's face. 'That gash across your cheek must have been particularly painful, wasn't it? It seems to be healing well but if you like, we'll send our personal physician across who is very good. In fact, his ointments did wonders for Zulfiqar Khan, whose own doctors had practically given up.'

'No, they are only some slight scratches,' replied Murad,

'Scratches you say? Anyone else with those wounds would have surrendered or fled from the battlefield. The way you deflected the spear hurled at you by that Rajput...what was his name...er...yes...Rup Singh and then shot him between the eyes has been the talk of the entire army. We didn't see it myself, as at that moment we were engaged in fending off attacks. But all who saw it said it was an act of supreme courage to have fought off all those Rajput warriors, who were swarming around you despite your wounds. They praised your good marksmanship too in felling Rup Singh with a single shot.'

Just then Aurangzeb clapped his hands. A servitor appeared at the other end of the pavilion and parted the curtains. Aurangzeb nodded. The man acknowledged the nod with a bow and withdrew.

'You too were no less brave,' replied Murad, attempting to be generous. 'And extremely magnanimous too. Sparing the life of that man who was trying to cut the girth of your elephant. Few would have done that.'

'Oh! That...' replied Aurangzeb dismissively. 'We belong to the house of Timur. If we know how to win battles, we also know how to spare the lives of those of our adversaries, who really distinguish themselves by their bravery.'

Just then the curtains parted and four extremely beautiful young girls, in the bloom of youth, came in bearing flagons of wine and several delicacies in trays, which they set on the table. Each of them was dressed in a flared silken kameez under a low-cut waistcoat worn tightly, which accentuated the gentle swell of their bust, and diaphanous harem pants which could barely conceal their generous curves. Tiny silver bells adorned their ankles, which tinkled with each step they took. Aurangzeb noticed Murad's eyes light up when he saw them.

'Where have you been hiding these houries, brother?' asked Murad. 'We never knew that Agra held such delectable beauties, otherwise we might have decided to...er...plan our visit much earlier.'

Aurangzeb just smiled. 'Call them the spoils of war,' he replied.

As one of the girls bent over to pour Murad some wine, he saw the gentle swell of her breasts and the perfume she exuded maddened his senses. With some difficulty he restrained himself, as he was in the presence of his elder brother. All this did not escape Aurangzeb's notice.

'Ah! Shirazi wine,' exclaimed Murad, as he watched the amber-coloured liquid being poured into the jewel-encrusted cup. 'We can make out its aroma from a distance. It is our favourite. We searched high and low for it in Gujarat, but could not find it. Where did you get it? Incidentally, its taste is enhanced if pearls are crushed in it.'

'It was one of the gifts brought by the Persian Ambassador, when he was newly accredited. The flagons were carried to Agra when the court moved there from Delhi and were lying unopened. Knowing that you liked this wine, we had brought a quantity of it with us, and yes, there are some of the finest Deccani pearls dissolved in it.'

'You think of everything, brother, don't you?' exclaimed Murad, as he drained his cup at one gulp and quickly held it out for another. One of the girls standing close by hastened to refill. Aurangzeb, who never touched liquor, unless for political reasons he was compelled to do so, lifted his own drinking cup to his lips, and when Murad was temporarily distracted, poured its contents into a nearby flowerpot.

'Now about those arrangements...' began Murad expansively.

Aurangzeb cut him short. 'Brother, why are you in such a hurry? We have all the time in the world. Neither of us is going anywhere. We assure you that the arrangements we have in mind will meet with your full approval. For the first time after that great battle, we have had the occasion to spend a few moments with each other. Let us make the most of it.'

'Oh, all right...it's just that this wine is so very good that we fear you may make us quite drunk before you tell us...tell us what arrangements you are contemplating.'

'We wouldn't dream of doing that,' murmured Aurangzeb, under his breath. Then aloud he said, 'Tell us about your hunting expedition.'

'Well, in two weeks we have bagged three tigers, a leopard, nineteen neelgai and countless deer and smaller animals. Two days ago, one of the tigers which we flushed out of the undergrowth, suddenly jumped onto the elephant we were riding and had practically reached upto the howdah. There was no time to reach for the musket and we had to despatch him with the sword. It was exhilarating to find the face of a snarling tiger barely four feet away. We hit him so hard that the blade cleaved the brute's skull. With a great howl, it fell back, losing its grip on the elephant and when we got down to make sure it was dead, the blade of my sword was still in the animal's brains. It shows that tigers too have brains.' Murad laughed at his little joke.

'Yes, that must have been really exciting,' remarked Aurangzeb, watching Murad who was now on his fourth cup of wine, but still did not seem to be any the worse for wear. No wonder his capacity to hold his liquor was legendary, Aurangzeb thought.

'We lost two beaters,' continued Murad. 'One of them was accidentally shot, when one of my officers heard some rustling in the bushes and fired at it, thinking him to be a deer. The other man was mauled by a leopard, which jumped on him from the branches of a tree where it was hiding. The poor fellow's neck was practically severed from the rest of his body, and half his entrails were hanging out when they took him away. Incidentally, the Raja of Devigarh has some wonderfully trained cheetahs for hunting.'

'Really,' replied Aurangzeb, feigning interest. 'What do they do?'

'He takes these cheetahs in covered carriages with a hood over their eyes. When they see a herd of antelopes grazing, the doors of the carriage are raised and the hood is removed. For a few moments, the cheetah sniffs the wind and generally as they are in the lee of the deer, those poor beasts have no idea what is about to strike them. The cheetah will stalk them through the grass or whatever cover the land provides, trying to get as close as possible, the very picture of concentration, and the moment the deer become aware of its presence and try to bolt, it gives chase. It is a sight to see the cheetah marking down an antelope, usually the weakest one in the herd, and moving in for the kill. The deer tries desperately bobbing and weaving to shake off its pursuer, but over short distances it is no match for the cheetah. One leap and the cheetah brings it down by raking its powerful claws into the haunches of the deer or sinking its teeth into its neck. A few last futile kicks and a couple of twitches later…the end. The cheetahs themselves are as docile as dogs and would not dream of running away. Once they bring down a deer, they have their faces hooded again and are then led back into their cages for the next sighting of deer.'

'Fascinating,' murmured Aurangzeb, as Murad was now on his fifth cup and a glazed look was coming into his eyes.

'Any news of brother Dara?' asked Murad, as he held out his empty cup for yet another refill. When he thought Aurangzeb was not looking, he carelessly, as if by accident, brushed his hand against the slave girl's rounded forearm. She did not attempt to withdraw it.

'The last reports that came in mentioned that he was near Lahore, hoping to suborn its killadar. He has a handful of men with him, and his speed is retarded by the presence of his wife and other ladies. We have given strict orders that anyone who opens his doors to him will answer personally to us with his head. In any case, Nasiri Khan is more than adequate to deal with him. Here, have another cup.' Aurangzeb motioned to the slave girl, who once again filled Murad's empty glass. By now Murad was draining the cup in single gulps.

'We never ccccould understand Ddddara,' slurred Murad. 'All that talk about finding common ground between different religions seems like sssssso much rubbissshhh. Each to his own religion, we say?'

'Nor can we countenance the fact that Dara has abandoned the true faith, and is chasing will of the wisps,' replied Aurangzeb fiercely. 'Common ground indeed! Does he want the ulema to lose faith in our dynasty and invite civil war so that this land which our forefathers won is made over to the non-believers? God willing, as long as there is breath left in our body, no opportunity will be given to him to spread his pernicious doctrines, and this land conquered by our forefathers will truly be made into a Darul Islam.'

'Well sssssspoken, brother. For us, Allah's word as contained in the Holy Koran is sufficient and it should be our endeavour to ensssshhhhure that this land which we have jointly won in battle and will jointly rule is made one which is truly worthy for all sincere believers.'

Aurangzeb's lips creased slightly in a sardonic smile, but he said nothing. So, dear brother you think we are going to rule jointly do you? Well you've got another guess coming.

By now, Murad was thoroughly drunk. He tried to stand, but lurched and fell heavily back onto the masnad, sending his goblet onto the floor and spilling all its contents onto the carpet. He looked at Aurangzeb with glazed eyes and smiled sheepishly. 'You musssshhhhht forgive us, brother. We seem to have had a little too much to drink.'

'Not at all,' said Aurangzeb. 'They say that the best antidote to an excess of wine is this particular distillation of herbs, which we have had specially procured. Here, have a sip of it.'

Aurangzeb poured out a green-coloured liquid from a small bottle from the table into a cup and held it out to Murad, who drank it at a single gulp but grimaced at its extremely bitter taste.

After some time, Murad said, 'Ah yes, we're feeling much better already.' His head had cleared to some extent and he tried to pick up the conversation where it had been left off. 'Now where were we? Oh, yes, our brothers. And what shall we do with our other brother, who also has royal pretensions?'

'That man?' asked Aurangzeb, scornfully. 'The stories we have heard about him would make anyone blush for shame. Woes betide that sad day, if such a man were to rule Hindustan. In any case, after his defeat at Sulaiman's hands, he will take considerable time to recover and both of us shall be ready for him.'

At these words, Murad puffed with pride. He had always

been in awe of his elder brother, and here was Aurangzeb, speaking of them jointly tackling Shuja. Could there be greater proof than this that Aurangzeb was willing to share the empire with him, and both would rule in a sort of condominium? Yet Murad, through the haze of intoxicating liquor, had some doubts. What if Aurangzeb made him only a junior partner, giving him all the inconvenient and secondary jobs, while he himself took all the great decisions? Would he have to play second fiddle all his life while Aurangzeb wrote his name in the history books? It was important to know what Aurngzeb had exactly in mind.

'You spoke just now of us facing Shuja together. What exactly do you have in mind?'

'Just what I said. We will face Shuja together,' replied Aurangzeb.

'After Shuja is defeated, what will be my role?'

'What role do you envisage for yourself?' asked Aurangzeb mildly.

Here is my chance, thought Murad. *It was now or never. Aurangzeb has given me an opening and we can take full advantage of it. Better to be the master of one's own principality than the second man in Agra or Delhi. True, our ambition was to become emperor of all Hindustan, but that would have to wait for a more opportune moment. For the present, partition of the empire between us and Aurangzeb seems like the best solution. After all was it not his resolute defence that eventually won us the victory in the decisive battle at Samugarh? More importantly, had not Aurangzeb himself in our correspondence hinted at partition?*

'As we may have difficulties ruling the empire together, we suggest we have an amicable partition in terms of your own indications to us when we were corresponding about our alliance,' replied Murad. *There! It had been ridiculously easy*, he thought.

'Partition' replied Aurangzeb, as if he was mulling over the word. Murad had half expected Aurangzeb to explode on hearing that word, and had braced himself for a long sustained argument, to defend his demand, but here was his elder brother taking the proposal with great mildness. 'And how do you propose that the empire be partitioned?'

'In accordance with your indications, roughly all the territories lying to the west of the river Indus fall to my share. The rest is yours,' replied Murad.

'Well, we think something can be worked out along those lines subject to marginal adjustments.'

'You agree?' asked Murad, incredulously. He could not believe his luck. He had been prepared for a massive struggle with his elder brother for his share of the empire, only to find that Aurangzeb had agreed to his demand without demur. He only wished he had asked for more; perhaps Gujarat. Then a faint whiff of suspicion crossed his mind. Aurangzeb seemed to have agreed too easily. Would he renege from the deal? Should he summon witnesses to attest what Aurangzeb had agreed to? That could perhaps be done later. Right now, it was important to get Aurangzeb to commit in writing what he had agreed to. Tomorrow, the agreement could be formally drawn up and attested by witnesses.

'Brother if we are agreed on this, let us commit it in writing, so that neither of us can then deny it later.'

'By all means,' said Aurangzeb. He clapped his hands and ordered the servant to fetch a scribe. The servant went out and later reappeared with a scribe in tow. Swiftly Aurangzeb dictated the terms of what had been agreed to, whereby the empire was to be partitioned; the subahs of Afghania, Kashmir, Punjab, Sindh and Tatta falling to the share of Murad and the rest to Aurangzeb. As the scribe finished the dictation and handed the scroll over to Aurangzeb, he was escorted out under armed guard and detained, lest he divulge to others what he had just heard and written. Later, if necessary, he would be quietly put to death, in what would be made to look like an accident, and his family would be generously compensated for their loss. Aurangzeb signed the scroll with a flourish.

'Would you like the agreement witnessed by two Qazis, to set it beyond all controversy? That too can be easily arranged,' he said, handing over the scroll to Murad.

'Let us leave that for the morrow,' replied Murad taking the quill held out by Aurangzeb and adding his own signature below that of his elder brother before putting the scroll into the inner pocket of his tunic. 'We must celebrate this really historical agreement. The Mughal empire is now entering upon its most glorious phase. You ruling in the east, and I in the west. You must expand the empire further south till our boundaries lap the waters of the southern seas, while for me limitlss opportunities lie towards the west—Iran to begin with, which is ripe for collapse and then...Baghdad...Khufa...Damascus and perhaps one day...who knows...even Mecca Sharif!'

Carried away by his own vision of uninterrupted victory, Murad waved his empty cup and one of the slave girls rushed to fill it. 'Come, brother, join us in this moment of history,' he said, as he drained the goblet at one gulp and asked for another.

Aurangzeb knew he had Murad just where he wanted him, but it was too early to play all his cards as yet. Better to make the man totally insensible through drink before putting his plan into operation. Steadily, he plied Murad with the fiery wine and saw him lose control of his senses.

'Wwwwon't ...you...keep us company?' stuttered Murad, as he tried to focus his eyes on Aurangzeb.

'Here we are, matching cup for cup with you,' replied Aurangzeb, as he threw the umpteenth cup of wine into the flowerpot, which now seemed to be brimming with it.

'You know, Dara had given us a totally wrong impression about you,' said Murad, becoming garrulous. 'Ever since childhood, Dara had made you out to be extremely narrow-minded, a killjoy, a bigot, crafty and deceitful and much else besides. We wish we had got to know each other better then, because we don't find you like that at all. Indeed, when we came to this meeting we were prepared for some hard bargaining, and we had not the slightest idea that matters would be settled so amicably as this. But remember one thing. Whatever your other brothers may say or do, this brother of yours will stick by you through thick and thin. We swear that by all that is holy.'

'We have no doubt about that,' muttered Aurangzeb.

As Murad babbled on, thoroughly drunk by this time, with Aurangzeb looking pityingly at him, he decided that the time was now ripe for putting the rest of the plan into operation. At a given signal, an aide came into the marquee to tell him that his presence was urgently required to settle a dispute between two powerful nobles of the court.

'You will excuse us. We shall be back as soon as this little matter is settled,' said Aurangzeb. 'Meanwhile please treat this camp as your own.'

Murad was now all alone in the marquee except for one of the slave girls, the most beautiful of them all, who had entered to serve him some more wine. The others had quietly withdrawn earlier, and Murad guessed that Aurangzeb had deliberately left so that he could be alone with the girl.

'What is your name, my beautiful one?' Murad asked.

'Aarzoo, Sire,' she replied in soft, dulcet tone of voice that semed to mesmerize Murad.

'How old are you and where do you hail from?'

'I have not seen eighteen summers, Sire, and my birthplace is across the mountains in Kashmir.'

'Ah, a name as pretty as your face, and your birthplace accounts for the peach-like bloom on your cheeks and the rosebud-like redness of your lips. Come sit by my side.' Murad gently drew her towards him. He knew that this superlatively beautiful girl was not to be ruthlessly violated as was his wont, but had to be savoured, slowly and delicately. Turning her face towards him, he planted a chaste kiss on her forehead and then his mouth travelled down to her lips. The smell of this coarse man's wine-laden breath on her mouth, which had never felt a man's lips before, made the poor girl nearly vomit. But she had been coached by Aurangzeb's chief eunuch as to exactly what she was to do, to release her parents from Aurangzeb's custody. She stifled her feelings and let Murad's hands travel all over her body, as he felt the gentle swell of her breasts under her bodice and clasped her slim waist.

'Subahnallah,' exclaimed Murad as he looked into the girl's eyes. 'No wonder they say that the valley of Kashmir is God's earthly paradise, if its inhabitants are so wonderously beautiful as you.'

'You are only too kind, Sire. If you will allow me, I shall transport you into flights of ecstacy which few mortals have experienced.'

'Ho, ho, ho,' laughed Murad. 'What has a girl like you who

has not even reached eighteen years got to teach?'

'Close your eyes, Sire,' she said, 'and give me your wrist.'

Murad closed his eyes and offered her his right wrist. From under the masnad where it had been kept concealed, the girl drew out a pair of golden handcuffs and swiftly clamped one end of it around Murad's wrist and the other end to one of the legs of the masnad.

Meanwhile with her soft hands she had unbuttoned Murad's tunic and was caressing his body. Eyes closed, Murad was in heavenly bliss, dreaming of how in a little while this enchantress would be completely his.

After a few moments, finding that her ministrations had ceased, he said, 'Now Aarzoo, we are going to open our eyes. Remove the handcuff so that we can know you better.'

As there was no response, he opened his eyes. Aarzoo was nowhere to be seen. Instead, to his utter shock, there was Aurangzeb with several nobles staring down at him as he lay sprawled on the masnad, legs apart, dishevelled, clothes undone and awry. He tried to stand but the handcuffs held him back.

'And this is the man who wants to rule the empire of Hindustan,' said Aurangzeb with the utmost contempt and derision. The nobles burst out into loud guffaws.

'Brother, what is this? Is this a game?' Murad snarled. 'If so it has been played long enough. Have these handcuffs removed at once. Can you countenance your own brother being humiliated in this fashion? Guards! Guards! Where are my guards?' Again he tried to rise, but fell back.

Aurangzeb ignored Murad's presence as if he did not even exist. Addressing the nobles who were peering down at the recumbent prince, he asked, 'If a man cannot even deal with the wiles of a seventeen-year-old girl, is he fit to rule an empire?'

'Certainly not, Sire,' they all cried in unison.

Turning to Murad, Aurangzeb said, 'You heard them? As for your guards, they are in our protective custody. Have no fear. They will be treated well.'

'But our agreement...' babbled Murad, incoherently. '...remember our agreement....the one we have just signed... with you ruling in the east and us in the west?' He reached out for the scroll he had placed inside his tunic, but it wasn't there. Furiously he patted his tunic with his free hand. 'It isn't there. It isn't there,' he muttered to himself, as he looked up at Aurangzeb. He drew a blank as Aarzoo had quietly removed it from his tunic while she was caressing him and had handed it over to Aurangzeb as she fled from the marquee.

'Agreement? What agreement? Do you think you are in a fit enough condition for us to sign any agreement with you?' asked Aurangzeb.

'The one we had just signed,' Murad screamed. 'You had called a scribe and had dictated the terms of the agreement according to which...'

Aurngzeb cut him short. 'What utter rubbish! Your brain remains clouded with opium and drink, and all this talk of an agreement is a figment of your hallucinations,' he said curtly. Then turning to the nobles assembled round the masnad, Aurangzeb once again said, 'As many of you are aware, this wretch has the blood of an innocent man on his hands. Our revered father had sent Ali Naqi as Diwan to Ahmedabad to straighten out the financial affairs of the province, and give good counsel to our brother here. What did our brother do? Instead of heeding that counsel, he ran his spear through the old man in broad daylight in the presence of witnesses, killing him instantly. Murdering with his own hands a high minister of the empire! Does not our faith teach us that to shed the blood of a single innocent man is to kill all humanity?'

Those assembled around the masnad nodded.

'Ten days ago,' continued Aurangzeb, 'the eldest son of Ali Naqi met us, and demanded as his price the blood of his father's murderer, in accordance with the laws of our faith. We told him that a ruling on an issue as important as this could be given only by a properly constituted court of Qazis, so that later on history would have no occasion to say that justice was not done. We, therefore, intend to produce this man before a court of Qazis at the earliest opportunity, who will pronounce their verdict on the grave crime committed by him and in the meantime he shall remain detained in our custody. We trust that this course of action meets with your approval.'

There was a murmur of approval among those present. None dared to dissent.

Beckoning Mohsin Khan, the Killadar of Salimgarh fort in Delhi, Aurangzeb said, 'Khan Saheb, we entrust the person of our brother Murad to your custody in Salimgarh. While in your custody he will be entitled to all the privileges and conveniences admissible to a prince of the blood, except that his movements will be restricted to the confines of his apartments within the fort and any person who seeks to meet him will have to be personally approved by us. He may choose such companions as he wishes to have for the duration of his custody provided that their number at any one time does not exceed…er…two… Guard him with your life.'

Mohsin Khan bowed and sprang forward to execute the command. A detachment of guards who were positioned just beyond the marquee entered, and Murad's ankles were bound in golden fetters whose chain was then passed around his wrists. 'You shall pay for this a hundredfold,' Murad roared before being led away. 'As long as there is life in us, we shall seek revenge. Don't for a moment think you will be able to get away with this.'

Aurangzeb scarcely bothered to throw a glance at his brother, as Murad was led away. One by one the assembled nobles bowed and took their leave. For a while, Aurangzeb sat all alone on the masnad under the marquee, running over in his mind all that had transpired in the last few hours. Then he walked to the entrance of the marquee and parted the curtains. Overhead the inky blackness of the night was giving way gradually, ever so gradually, to a grey darkness, while the first streaks of dawn were lightening the sky in the east. Slowly the great camp was coming to life. Yes, it promised to be a bright morning.

Epilogue

THE OLD MAN laid his head on the austere pallet that was his bed in Aurangbad. As he stretched out his gaunt, pain-wracked frame upon it, and peered into the darkness of the Deccan night, running his fleshless fingers through the straggly beard that rested on his chest, sleep eluded Aurangzeb Alamgir, Emperor of Hindustan. Gone was the man of implacable will and iron discipline, the king who the Uzbegs claimed that to fight was to invite self destruction, one whose mere frown made potenates tremble. In his place was a man, old and frail, who was human after all, and heir to all the infirmities and querulousness of one who had lived to sustain the burden of eighty-nine summers.

Like many nights in the past, the old demons hovering around his bedside had come to haunt him—the memories, the doubts, the utter loneliness. Would he never receive surcease from their torments? But did he deserve any respite, when he had blighted the lives of so many who had come within his reach? Figures from years gone by presented themselves like images in a kaleidoscope to form, dissolve and reform again in a different shape—his own father incarcerated by him in Agra fort and dying by inches as he himself was doing now; Dara betrayed and brought to Delhi in chains, where clad in beggar's garments and seated on a grime-encrusted elephant he was paraded through its streets to the lamentations of its people on seeing their prince so humiliated, till he was hastily executed; Shuja fleeing into the Arakan forests after his defeat by Mir Jumla and murdered by the local ruler along with his son Zain; Murad, that gallant fool who fought with lion-hearted courage when the fate of the Mughal empire hung in the balance, only to be undone by the oldest strategem in the world, eventually losing his life in a dungeon in Gwalior; Murad's son, by that beauteous Circassian slave girl who died during childbirth. The boy inherited his father's courage and his mother's light eyes and fought in Aurangzeb's army, dying heroically, a mere stripling, before his uncle's stern gaze in the assault on Golconda; Udaipuri Mahal, the only woman he had ever loved and mother of his favourite son Mohammed Kam Baksh, was herself old and still in her grave; and scores of others.

All the battles, the bloodshed, the treachery, the accompanying heat, dust, famine and pestilence that had gone into wresting the empire lest it fell into unworthy hands, safeguarding it and then extending its frontiers—had it all been worth it? Or had his life been a monumental failure, with the Marathas still unsubdued in their mountain fastnesses in the Deccan, despite twenty years of campaigning, rebellion raising its head elsewhere and even his own sons ranged against him? Would they do to him, as he lay weak and dying, what he had done to them and to his own father? And what about those faceless millions who had drowned in a vale of tears during his rule? Would their imprecations follow him to the grave?

It was strange that he, who had come into the world with nothing, was about to depart with this enormous caravan of sins. Was repentance possible even at this stage? But who would intercede for him before Allah on Judgement Day? Would it not have been better if he had continued to tread the path of a fakir, which he had once chosen, to commune all alone with God, instead of coming back into the world of men in order to rule them? But then who could alter what had been written in the Great Book? It was his destiny to be the ruler of the Mughal empire at its moment of greatest expansion, and as God's humble servant he had only tried to do his duty by upholding and extending the true faith. Who could change what was foreordained?

When had it all begun? he asked himself, as his eyelids gradually dropped in merciful sleep. *Thirty years ago? Forty years ago? No, perhaps it all began that day nearly half a century ago, when Emperor Shah Jahan was taken ill…*